10/11

ARCHITECTURAL DESIGN

D0809510

UEST-EDITED BY
aDRIAN LAHOUD,
CHARLES RICE AND
aNTHONY BURKE

POST-TRAUMATIC
URBANISM

05|2010

aRCHITECTURAL DESIGN
VOL 80, NO 5
SEPTEMBER/OCTOBER 2010
ISSN 0003-8504

PROFILE NO 207
ISBN 978-0470-744987

WILEY
wiley.com

ARCHITECTURAL DESIGN

GUEST-EDITED BY
ADRIAN LAHOUD,
CHARLES RICE AND
ANTHONY BURKE

POST-TRAUMATIC URBANISM

78

64

ARCHITECTURAL DESIGN
SEPTEMBER/OCTOBER 2010
PROFILE NO 207

Editorial Offices
John Wiley & Sons
25 John Street
London
WC1 N2BS

T: +44 (0)20 8326 3800

Editor
Helen Castle

Freelance Managing Editor
Caroline Ellerby

Production Editor
Elizabeth Gongde

Design and Prepress
Artmedia, London

Art Direction and Design
CHK Design:
Christian Küsters
Hannah Dumphy

Printed in Italy by Conti Tipocolor

Sponsorship/advertising
Faith Pidduck/Wayne Frost
T: +44 (0)1243 770254
E: fpidduck@wiley.co.uk

Subscribe to AD

AD is published bimonthly and is available to purchase on both a subscription basis and as individual volumes at the following prices.

Prices
Individual copies: £22.99/$45.00
Mailing fees may apply

Annual Subscription Rates
Student: UK£70/US$110 print only
Individual: UK £110/US$170 print only
Institutional: UK£180/US$335
print or online
Institutional: UK£198/US$369
combined print and online

Subscription Offices UK
John Wiley & Sons Ltd
Journals Administration Department
1 Oldlands Way, Bognor Regis
West Sussex, PO22 9SA
T: +44 (0)1243 843272
F: +44 (0)1243 843232
E: cs-journals@wiley.co.uk

[ISSN: 0003-8504]

Prices are for six issues and include postage and handling charges. Periodicals postage paid at Jamaica, NY 11431. Air freight and mailing in the USA by Publications Expediting Services Inc, 200 Meacham Avenue, Elmont, NY 11003.
Individual rate subscriptions must be paid by personal cheque or credit card. Individual rate subscriptions may not be resold or used as library copies.

All prices are subject to change without notice.

Postmaster
Send address changes to Publications Expediting Services Inc, 200 Meacham Avenue, Elmont, NY 11003

Rights and Permissions
Requests to the Publisher should be addressed to:
Permissions Department
John Wiley & Sons Ltd
The Atrium
Southern Gate
Chichester
West Sussex PO19 8SQ
England

F: +44 (0)1243 770620
E: permreq@wiley.co.uk

Front cover: Zoriah Miller, War Photography, Gaza, 2006. The rubble of a former settlement in the Gaza Strip, 28 April 2006. © Zoriah Miller, www.zoriah.com
Inside front cover: Unidad Residencial 2 de Diciembre, Caracas, c 1960. © Fundación Villanueva, photo Paolo Gasparini, Archivo Funcación Villanueva. Design by CHK Design.

This issue opens elegiacally with an introduction by guest-editor Adrian Lahoud that evokes recent events in the tenor of a science-fiction narrative, summoning up a post-apocalyptic world that has already happened. This is a world that has had a consistent scattering of natural disasters and conflicts – the Pacific tsunami, 9/11, the Afghan war, occupation of Iran, Hurricane Katrina, the Shenzhen and Haiti earthquakes – to name but a few that have captured the international media's attention. This raises important questions as to the relationship that architectural design and architectural thought might have with the urban rubble of reality at a time when the dominant cultural thrust in leading architectural schools and cutting-edge practices remains focused on the synthetic smooth and complex surfaces made possible by the parametric. This issue effectively does this by tapping into another equally current, but alternative thrust in architecture – that of architectural research through fieldwork, which has become increasingly dominant since the mid-1990s when Rem Koolhaas launched the Project in the City programme at Harvard and made China's Pearl River Delta and Lagos the subjects of his widely published enquiries. This tendency to study often extreme urban conditions has become prevalent in leading architectural schools that offer international programmes and off-site trips to their students; certainly it was apparent this summer in London at the Bartlett School of Architecture's and the Architectural Association's shows where a large portion of units' work had been underpinned by fieldwork undertaken in places as diverse as Tenerife and Eastern Europe to Dubai and US highways. In this issue we see this tendency heightened by architectural research projects into urban conditions that are recovering from the aftermath of manmade and natural crises whether it is the Lebanon Civil War in Beirut or the earthquake in Shenzhen. Significant philosophers such as Andrew Benjamin, Brian Massumi and Slavoj Žižek engage with the discussion by contributing ideas behind the notion of urban trauma. This leads to important questions over what architects can learn from studying urban conditions in their most fragile, raw and unstable state. Lahoud, in his introduction, urges for inquiry while stressing that 'architects do not heal trauma' and can indeed be 'complicit with its production'. Through this type of inquiry, what might architects potentially contribute to cities in the aftermath of conflict or natural disaster? Should we be encouraging or discouraging this type of engagement, which often leads architectural students and inexperienced young architects to rush off, in a heartfelt response, to New Orleans or Haiti to 'help out'. Jayne Merkel's and Craig Whitaker's article for the Counterpoint series of 𝝙, which offers established voices in architecture the opportunity to challenge the main theme of the issue, here controversially argues that in these extreme situations 'international architectural talent and expertise are irrelevant – even undesirable'. Can architects only ever have the best interests of the greater population in mind with a clear understanding that human tragedy is not inevitably architectural opportunity?

Adrian Lahoud, Tripoli Masterplan, Lebanon, 2010
top left: This project for the city of Tripoli in Lebanon begins with a traumatic blind spot. The blind spot forms in the space once occupied by Oscar Niemeyer's proposal for a fair and expo site. The trauma the blind spot conceals is not some violent aspect of the civil war in Lebanon but the disappearance of the future epitomised by the progressive, experimental drive of the project. This ongoing project explores possibilities for rehabilitating the site by stimulating economic activity along the perimeter.

John Portman and Associates, Hyatt Regency, San Francisco, 1973
top right: Rice's new research considers the effects of large atrium spaces on the emergence of interior urbanism in the context of development opportunities in North American downtowns from the late 1960s.

Offshore Studio Pty Ltd, Bonehouse, 2006
above: Burke's Offshore Studio is a design research practice focusing on the intersection of information and organisational systems and their impact on contemporary architectural design. The Bonehouse project has been widely published and exhibited in Beijing, San Francisco and Sydney.

As colleagues in the School of Architecture at the University of Technology in Sydney (UTS), Adrian Lahoud (Master of Advanced Architecture, Urban Design), Charles Rice (Associate Professor) and Anthony Burke (Associate Professor and Head of School) have developed an approach to urban research which recognises the city as an unstable, though highly organised, environment. The particular theme of this issue of ∆ allows this research to frame trauma and its aftermath as the most current and widely understood manifestation of urban instability.

As a practising architect and Course Director of the Master of Advanced Architecture, Urban Design, Lahoud's work ranges across a number of scales with a particular emphasis on the Middle East. As a researcher he explores the relationship between design, conflict and politics. He is a member of the OCEAN design research network and is completing a doctorate entitled 'The Life of Forms in the City'.

Rice's research considers the interior as a spatial and experiential category in domestic and urban culture. His book *The Emergence of the Interior: Architecture, Modernity, Domesticity* was published by Routledge in 2007, and he is currently working on a book manuscript provisionally titled *Atrium Effects: John Portman and Architecture's Discipline*. Here he will consider how questions of urban renewal have, since the 1970s, been linked to particular design strategies which emphasise heightened interior effects. With current thinking and practice so focused on the envelope, climate control and security, thinking through the increasing interiority of urbanism has become a pressing issue.

Burke's research addresses questions of computational media and technology, and its implications for architecture and urbanism. A graduate of Columbia University's GSAPP in 2000, he has focused in particular on networks and systems logics within contemporary design, recently co-editing *Network Practices: New Strategies in Architecture and Design* (Princeton Architectural Press, 2007) with Therese Tierney. His practice, Offshore Studio, like Lahoud's practice, works across scales to test this research-led design thinking.

In this issue of ∆, Lahoud, Rice and Burke aim to wed design experimentation to politics. Their day-to-day collaboration in research and teaching promotes the consideration of advanced techniques, criticality and the reality of the urban together as the context for architecture's disciplinary development. ∆

The editors would like to thank Diana Hanna Hani for her invaluable assistance in preparing this issue of ∆.

from above: Adrian Lahoud, Charles Rice and Anthony Burke

SPOTLIGHT

Diana Hanna Hani,
Farouk Kork, Hugh Irving,
Samaneh Moafi, Grace Uy
and Tobias Robinson

Continuity, Social Transformations Studio (tutors: Adrian Lahoud and Samantha Spurr), University of Technology, Sydney, 2008
One of the projects undertaken by the Social Transformation Studio at the University of Technology, Sydney, that has based workshops in Shenzhen, Berlin and Beirut (see pp 50–7), this proposal by a group of students for the suburb of Bachoura in Beirut carefully maps and documents social and cultural issues, highlighting the importance of continuity for an ancient city wrought by internal conflict for so many years.

The post-traumatic city as a subject of inquiry necessitates leaving the notion of the architectural palimpsest behind. As represented here through designs and studies for areas as diverse as Beirut, the Ganges River Corridor in India and the Gulf of Mexico, the built environment becomes the site for mapping, reframing and careful projection informed by past and current contexts.

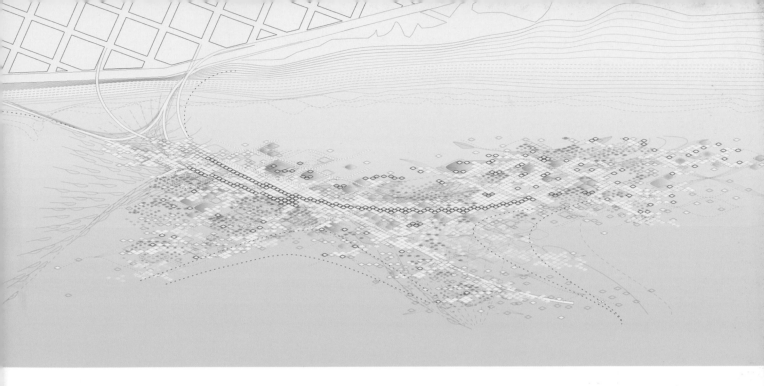

←

↑

↓

**Erik Escalante +
Alina McConnochie**

**Nkiru Mokwe and
Viktor Ramos**

**Erik Escalante +
Alina McConnochie**

**Master of Architecture, Social
Transformations Studio (tutors: Adrian
Lahoud and Samantha Spurr), University
of Technology Sydney, 2009**
Infrastructure and transport are pivotal
for connecting cities and reconfiguring
urban development. Here, Masters'
students at Sydney speculate the
transformative impact of a high-speed
rail network extending across the
Mediterranean and into the Middle East.

**Energe(ne)tic Fields,
Last Resorts Studio, 2007**
The Last Resorts design studio at the Rice
School of Architecture focuses its fieldwork
on Galveston Island, which was devastated
by Hurricane Ike. This offers students
the unique opportunity to work with a
coastal engineer and geologist in an area of
extreme coastal erosion.

**Beirut City Extension: Imperfect
Difference, Incomplete Repetition, Social
Transformations Studio (tutors: Adrian
Lahoud and Samantha Spurr), University
of Technology, Sydney, 2009**
A futuristic but 'imperfect' high-
performance extension is envisaged here
for the existing city.

Fadi Mansour

**Re-Framing the City: A Monument of Radical Neutrality, AA Diploma Unit 6
(tutors: Chris Lee and Sam Jacoby), Architectural Association, London, 2009**
In this project for the Green Line in Beirut, which separated Muslim West Beirut from
Christian East Beirut during the Lebanese Civil War, an architecture is created with an
entirely new programme for a public institution – a Lebanese university accessible to
all ethnic groups and factions in the community. This manifests itself spatially in the
form of a void that monopolises the site of the last neutral ground in the city.

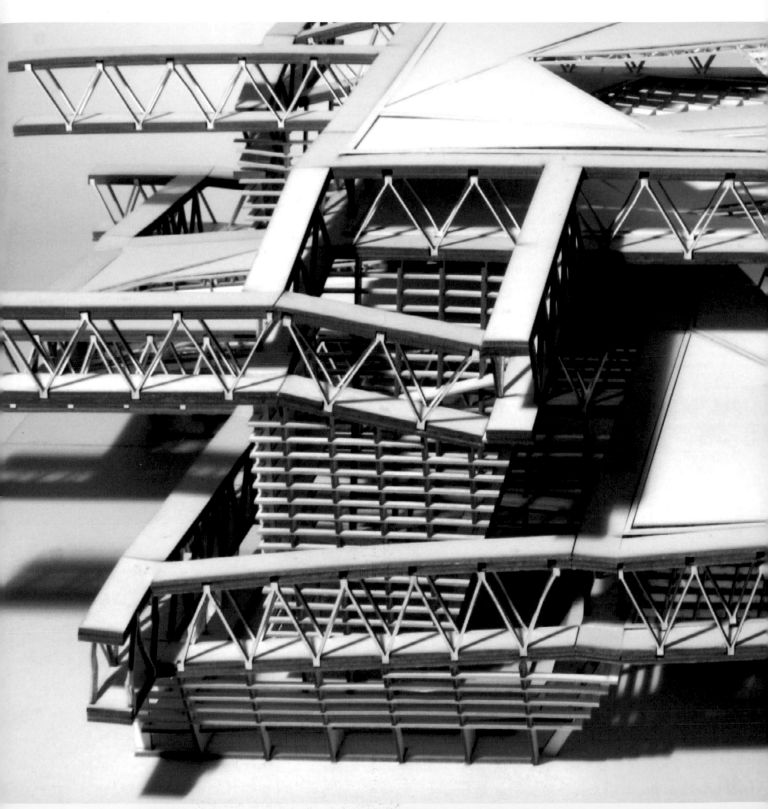

Anthony Acciavatti

Dynamic Atlas, India Ganges, 2006
Acciavatti's 'Dynamic Atlas' series of drawings measure the effects of rainfall and processes on urbanisation in the River Ganges Corridor in northern India, emphasising the extreme perennial changes that the region undergoes with the annual monsoon season from late June to August.

POST-TRAUMATIC URBANISM

At 9:03 am on 11 September 2001, the protective membrane that sealed the third world from the first was punctured by the spear point of United Airlines Flight 175. Only 17 minutes earlier, the first plane set the stage. Now the second aircraft – a re-enactment of the first – immediately turned a singular catastrophe into an apocalyptic performance. The direct result was a crisis of political insulation. The core could no longer protect itself against terrors long familiar to the periphery and the frontier. Four years later, Mississippi floodwaters filled the breach. The culpable abandonment of its citizens by the world's only superpower made the privileges of first-world membership look fragile. In the embryonic moments of the post-traumatic age, the third world penetrates the first with tendrils of fear and insecurity. What was once far grows unbearably close.

This issue of ᗞ asks what mappings are possible between the optimism of experimentation and the critical situations we find ourselves in. It is a question that attempts to redirect the creative impulse of the avant-garde towards problems that are both current and relevant and thus finds its exemplary figure in urban trauma and its aftermath.

Urbanism is parasitic on crisis. Crisis is productive. Threats – both real and imagined – fill its veins and flesh out its form. This issue of ᗞ refuses to

Martin Abbott, Georgia Herbert, Clare Johnston, Joshua Lynch, Alexandra Wright, The Diversity Machine and the Resilient Network, Social Transformations Studio (tutors: Adrian Lahoud and Samantha Spurr), University of Technology, Sydney, 2009
The project speculates on the emancipatory potential of a high-speed rail network linking countries in a future Mediterranean Union, asking the question: What are the transformational effects of infrastructure on the post-traumatic context of Beirut?

frame trauma in terms that are moral, messianic or apocalyptic. This means guillotining most discourse on the environment, ecology, conflict and humanitarian aid. Architects do not heal trauma; they are complicit with its production. What is required is an unsentimental inquiry into the conditions we are being presented with, an inquiry that does not seek to motivate action through the production of fear.[1]

To begin with, what does it mean to raise the word 'urbanism' alongside the word 'trauma'? What is the point of taking a word that is already contentious in psychoanalytic theory and holding it up against a term like urbanism? It would not be to claim that the built environment has some unconscious that suffers; rather, the point is to redistribute those questions we take to be relevant and important with regards to urbanism. Urbanism is an open cipher upon which various other terms – 'reform', 'infrastructure', 'sustainability' or 'innovation' – make different demands. In each case, the questions that we take to be important with regards to cities are reorganised. Whereas one might imagine a discipline or field called sustainable urbanism, or infrastructural urbanism, there will never be a subdiscipline of 'post-traumatic urbanism' because trauma is that which exceeds systematisation. Trauma is by definition an exception, a collection of singularities.

The sting in history's tail is the profound unreliability of the past as a test for the future. The traumatic moment is unheralded and unprecedented.

Post-traumatic urbanism will have no manifesto, no canon and no adherents. This issue is a disruption to 'crisis as usual'. We ask: what new questions might emerge by raising the term urbanism alongside trauma? To elaborate on this, it is first necessary to take a moment to construct a definition of trauma that can survive its leap from a psychoanalytic domain to an urban one.

Our sensory apparatus and capacity for sense-making is constructed over time through the actions of repetition and habit. Every day we are provoked and lured by problems to which we gradually learn to adapt. This slow accumulation of impressions shapes our conception of the world and the potential of our agency within it.

Both evolutionary history and personal experience prime us to prepare ourselves for uncertainty in different ways. Each adopts a disposition or stance towards the future that draws on remembered progressions of both regular and exceptional events and their aftermath. The contractile in-gathering of memories orients out in a projectile vision of the future.

These events, which form the fundamental structuring stimuli of our sensory apparatus and capacity for sense-making, fall within a certain range or bandwidth of duration and intensity. Over time this seemingly random scattering of events begins to exhibit forms of regularity. The condensation of points around certain types of attractors reveals patterns of solicitation and response that we use to regulate our expectations of change. There is a connective synthesis at work here, a sort of rhythmic entrainment where processes of feedback and reinforcement begin to strengthen the bonds between constellations of distributed points.

These collections, which form the contours of our experiential landscape, describe a dynamic, complex, open system whose remarkable capacity for adaptation emerges out of the tension between the economies of repetition and the provocation of difference. If our tendencies tend to harden and our predispositions tend to ossify, it is mostly because a little risk has more evolutionary advantage than too much or none at all. It is why fear is such a potent and yet inherently conservative motor for action. And it is precisely why one should be wary of all those who are parasitic on crisis and feed on insecurity.

It is not the intention here to uncover the archaeological history of these repetitions that so organise our present; this has been carried out before. Rather it is to simply point out that this distribution describes a more or less delimited space or terrain and most importantly that the limits and topography of this space structure our capacity to absorb or locate new events as they arise. Because we rely on past events to calculate future ones, and because the sum total of our experience cannot exhaust the sum total of all possible experience, a space opens up beyond the horizons of our conceptual geography, a gap between what is historically accumulated and what is in fact possible. Beyond this horizon we find only the silence of as yet unnameable events.

The sting in history's tail is the profound unreliability of the past as a test for the future. The traumatic moment is unheralded and unprecedented. Classical causality is complicated by pre-emption. It arrives unrecognisably and without warning, an inassimilable event that shatters the very coordinates of our experiential landscape, leaving us adrift on a sea of excessive sensation. In the moment of trauma you are exiled from your own psychic landscape, a foreign intruder in an unfamiliar land.

Ordos, New City, China, 2010
Projects such as Ordos in Inner Mongolia in China crystallise the volatile and ethically fraught nexus between financial liquidity, real-estate speculation and the aesthetic currency of avant-garde architectural practice.

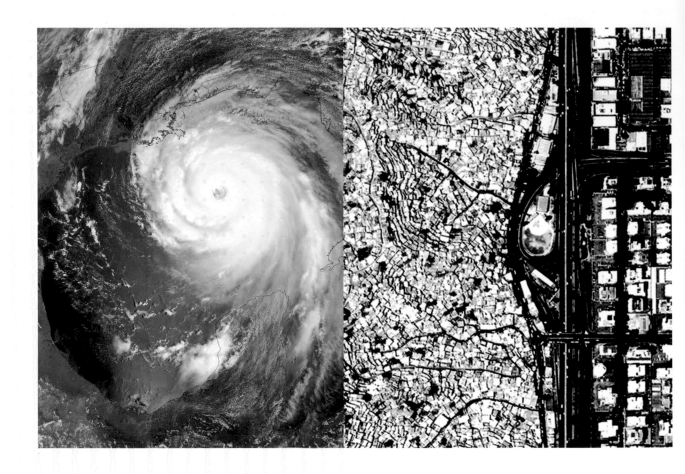

The term 'post-traumatic' refers to the evidence of the aftermath – the remains of an event that are missing. The spaces around this blind spot record the impression of the event like a scar.

NASA, Hurricane Katrina approaching the US Gulf Coast, 2005
above left: The aftermath of Hurricane Katrina seems to have crystallised a series of contemporary concerns relating to governance, corporatisation of aid work, social justice, racism, global warming and neoliberalism. That a disaster such as this could have an impact on thinking in such a diverse set of arenas is a testament to both the abject failure of the state to adequately support its citizens and to the renewed politicisation of 'natural' events. The urban politics that might yet emerge from this entangled environment where hydrological and meteorological conditions conspire to reorganise the distribution of people according to race or class, and proceed to refashion the very form of our cities, is one we may not yet recognise. Tracking and controlling the maturation of these infant technopolitical assemblages is a critical part of ensuring that these development drivers produce forms of urbanity that are guided by socially just and equitable politics.

La Vega + Petare y La Urbina, Caracas, Venezuela, 2005
above right: Aerial view of the discontinuity between formal and informal patterns. Infrastructure severs the emergent logic of the informal urban fabric from the centrally planned rationality of the city grid. This interruption or barrier to the growth of each system intensifies the differentiation between them. Rather than being understood as wounds to be healed or stitched over, the cuts or blockages in a city can also be simply seen as productive of difference so that the reflective impulse of reconnection can be examined.

Dahiyeh, Beirut, Lebanon, 2006
opposite: Aftermath of the Israeli invasion. In 2006, Israeli bombing destroyed much of Beirut's southern suburbs. By displacing the largely Shia population from these areas, Israel hoped to destabilise the internal political balance within Lebanon using an urban design strategy delivered by bunker busters and directed towards neighbourhood clearance. After the bombing, the internal climate was politically charged as different groups argued over the design of the proposed reconstruction and the degree to which it would repeat the urban plan of the destroyed neighbourhood. Design options were understood as means to establish historical continuity and embody different sorts of tactical potential.

Trauma forms an epistemological blind spot, a limit space behind which known experience recedes. This is why there is another name for trauma: 'the new'. In some sense the traumatic event is excessively new.[2] Human anticipation works by leaning slightly forward, meaning we can guess, make a small leap, infer and intuit. When these expectations are denied, and yet events still fall within a familiar series, we may be pleasantly surprised. However, when such events arrive from outside of any recognisable space they place the system under an intolerable strain. Trauma names that moment after our image of the future is destroyed but before it has been replaced.

> Now, in the months following the attacks, it is as if we are living in the unique time between a traumatic event and its symbolic impact, as in those brief moments after we have been deeply cut, before the full extent of the pain strikes us.
> — Slavoj Žižek, *Welcome to the Desert of the Real*, 2002, p 44[3]

The term 'post-traumatic' refers to the evidence of the aftermath – the remains of an event that are missing. The spaces around this blind spot record the impression of the event like a scar. How does a system make sense of an experience that exceeds its capacity for integration? Since recognition is only ever retroactive, the process of reintegrating the event, of sense-making, begins when we start to sift through the evidence, to build a plausible story, to construct a narrative and develop the coordinates of a new experiential landscape. Slowly repetition returns to weave its supportive tissue, and new futures come to replace old ones.

Trauma is the drama in which both history and the future are at stake, held in a suspended crisis; the cards have been thrown up in the air but they have not yet landed. Trauma stages the point at which the system must reimagine itself or perish.

Another term can be introduced to account for the possibility of action in this context: 'resilience'. If the twin poles of continuity/repetition and discontinuity/trauma form two asymptotic tendencies, resilience describes the ability to move between them. Resilience is the ability of a system to recover after it has absorbed some shock. Recovery, however, is never a simple return to its previous state of periodic repetition. After absorbing a shock, the resilient system creatively explores and trials new forms of stability. Some form of continuity is central here (we must reiterate our distance from the idea of a tabula rasa). Resilience is never a return, but it is never quite a full break either; though it leaps over interruption, it carries with it the continuity of a historical charge that lends it adaptive strength.

We are now in a position to give a provisional answer to the question that was asked earlier; what new demands would be made of urbanism by raising it alongside the term trauma? To begin with it would mean augmenting design discourse focused on optimisation with ideas that are calibrated to crisis, such as adaptation and resilience. A resilient city is one that has evolved in an unstable environment and developed adaptations to deal with uncertainty. Typically these adaptations take the form of slack and redundancy in its networks. Diversity and distribution, be they spatial, economic, social or infrastructural, will be valued more highly than centralised efficiency.

The post-traumatic city challenges all cybernetic theories of information flow and computation since it argues that these apparatuses of knowledge and calculation always imply the coexistence of blind spots, especially for the hubristic application of quantitative methods to qualitative domains. Further, the pre-emptive, the pre-traumatic and the post-traumatic are nothing less than the invention of new and highly complex scales and temporalities, where past and future durations intermingle and where short instantaneous traumas (violence, conflict) nest within glacial ones (climate change, environmental degradation). Finally, post-traumatic urbanism suggests that we know most about something when it breaks down, when it withdraws its invisible support and enters into the domain of all those things that can be interrupted, threatened and destroyed.

This issue of △ gathers together a diverse range of contributors, among them: Andrew Benjamin, Tony Chakar, Michael Chertoff, Mark Fisher, Brian Massumi, Todd Reisz, Eyal Weizman, and Slavoj Žižek, in order to draw into proximity the singular points of the post-traumatic city. It is worth introducing some of these arguments as they mark out the conceptual terrain of the issue. The central imaginary space of the city's future is cinema. If all generations have their dark spectres, ours is defined by the collective annihilation of urban space. Given that we are constantly rehearsing our own demise in widescreen, the question must be asked: is our projective fantasy a paranoid defence mechanism, repeating in advance what we fear most, or is the repetition of catastrophe a sign of some deeper malaise? In 'Post-Apocalypse Now' (pages 70–3), Mark Fisher argues that contemporary cinema expresses capitalism's hegemonic hold on our imagination. Recalling the claim that 'it is easier to imagine the end of the world than it is to imagine the end of capitalism', Fisher takes three recent films: *Children of Men*, *Terminator Salvation* and *The Road* as symptomatic of a contemporary state of ideological ruination that can only find expression in the devastated landscapes of recent cinema.

The image of ecological catastrophe is continually mobilised in environmental discourse. It is now a cliché to enlist images of disaster as support for urban arguments. Given that few rational people would argue with climate change, we should enquire as to why there is such massive cultural inertia when it comes to implementing sustainable strategies, and whether the portentous images of crisis challenge this immobility or secretly sustain it. Slavoj Žižek, in his interview on pages 112–15, argues that there is a disavowed economy to many of the conventional assumptions we make about sustainability. Žižek also argues that the political import of objects such as infrastructure is inherently open to contestation, and that we should take a pragmatic and opportunistic disposition to their potential appropriation.

Though post-apocalyptic cinema suggests that the only two possible inhabitants of the post-traumatic city are the 'suspect' and the 'survivor', both these characters might be better understood by referring to the figure of 'the unaccustomed'. In 'Trauma Within the Walls' (pages 24–31), Andrew Benjamin suggests that trauma is foundational to the city and democracy in that it provokes both with radical unfamiliarity. This 'unaccustomed' element stages an encounter with democracy that must respond by attempting to master this foreign presence. This encounter always threatens to spill into violence or assimilation; in either case the unfamiliar is neutralised and the city is deprived of the demand to negotiate difference.

The image of ecological catastrophe is continually mobilised in environmental discourse. It is now a cliché to enlist images of disaster as support for urban arguments.

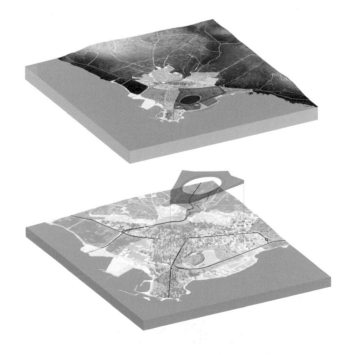

Adrian Lahoud, Insulation for Lost Optimism, Plan for the Rehabilitation of the Rachid Karame Fair and Exposition Site, Tripoli, Lebanon, 2010
opposite: The 1960s project for a fair and exposition site by Oscar Niemeyer for the city of Tripoli in Lebanon inscribes a perfect ellipse of 3.6 kilometres (2.2 miles) circumference on to the edge of the existing city fabric. Built at a time of unmediated optimism in the transformational and progressive potential of Modern architecture, the site now lies partially abandoned and neglected. Burdened by poor integration with its surrounding neighbourhoods, the unoccupied site forms a blind spot at the scale of a city, a blank space for fantasy and projection. This project proposes a ring of development along the perimeter of the blind spot so as to insulate the interior from exploitative uses and stimulate economic development along its periphery.

Diana Hanna Hani, Hugh Irving, Farouk Kork, Samaneh Moafi, Tobias Robinson and Grace Uy, Bachoura Master Plan, Social Transformations Studio (tutors: Adrian Lahoud and Samantha Spurr), University of Technology, Sydney, 2008
below: This proposal, undertaken in collaboration with the staff and students of the American University of Beirut, for the redevelopment of a site on the fringe of the renovated Beirut Central District (BCD) looks to architectural typology as a way of mediating the effects of gentrification on social and economic diversity. The question to be answered here – Is there a spatial equivalent to the concept of biodiversity in ecology? – implies that if spatial diversity has some relation to social diversity, these ecologies of building types will have the potential to provide niches for diverse forms of business and inhabitation while avoiding the homogeneity of the BCD or a tabula rasa approach to the existing context.

Martin Abbott, Georgia Herbert, Clare Johnston, Joshua Lynch and Alexandra Wright, The Diversity Machine and the Resilient Network, Social Transformations Studio (tutors: Adrian Lahoud and Samantha Spurr), University of Technology, Sydney, 2009
below: The project speculates on the emancipatory potential of a high-speed rail network linking countries in the Mediterranean Union, asking the question: What are the transformational effects of infrastructure on the city of Beirut? Beirut is a resilient, heterogenous city poised on the cusp of new waves of development. The resilience in its current urban condition is enabled by a system that encourages redundancy within small city networks. This redundancy allows for flexibility in the system, allowing it to creatively respond to obstructions and shocks caused by conflict. The resilient DNA of the existing urban fabric is decoded and redeployed around the proposed infrastructure in this new extension to the city.

Robert Beson, The Ruins of Modernism, Disciplinary Transformation Studio (tutor: David Burns), University of Technology, Sydney, 2009
opposite: Trauma is unknowable; it is the violator of systems including those of knowledge. As such it is only visible through the evidence it leaves on its surroundings.

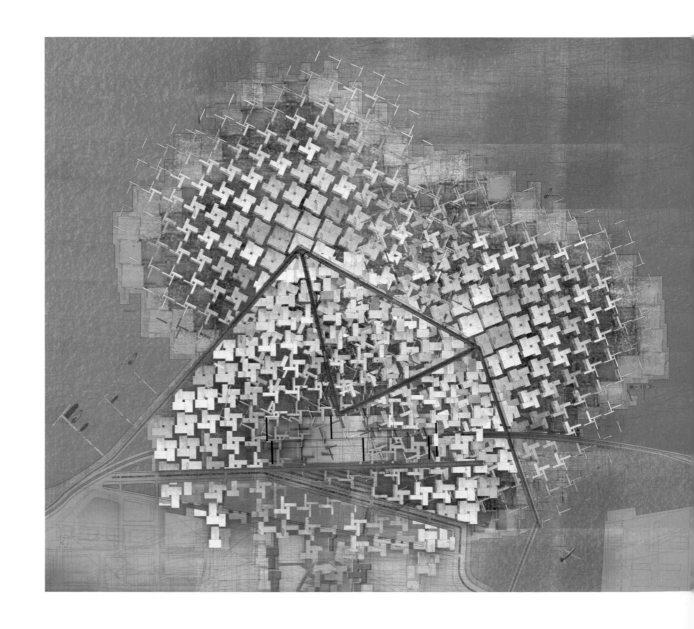

'The Eighth Day' (pages 74–7), by Tony Chakar, suggests that we can only ever describe the evidence that surrounds the catastrophic blind spot, because the event itself is inscrutable. Based on the Lebanese Civil War and its repetitions, Chakar describes the ruin of all representation in the aftermath of war. Objects, words, numbers all fail to refer to the same thing as before. Factual discourse becomes hollowed out and empty, frustrating the possibility of communication. Chakar argues that in the postwar context, nothing less than new modes of speaking must be invented.

Crises need image management. Public perception comes to structure the response to disaster and conflict to such an extent that highly sophisticated media strategies must be prepared in its anticipation. The production and manipulation of perceptions has direct implications for policy making and resource allocation in the aftermath of a major traumatic event. Michael Chertoff, former US Secretary of Homeland Security under President George W Bush, and now head of the crisis management venture the Chertoff Group and consultant to public relations company Burson-Marsteller, discusses pre-emptive strategies for media management in times of crisis in his interview with Charles Rice (pages 124–5). Chertoff suggests that the 'lessons learned' from both 9/11 and Hurricane Katrina have significantly altered approaches to risk management. In 'Making Dubai: A Process in Crisis' (pages 38–43), Todd Reisz recounts the post-crash climate after the collapse of the real-estate speculation market there, and the effort of public relations consultants in trying to resuscitate the image of the city. He suggests that behind the traffic of images, something more complex and long term is evolving in the Gulf state.

The aftermath haunts the present. As Brian Massumi explains in his interview with Charles Rice (pages 32–7), we feel the effects of the aftermath before the event arrives. The prefix 'post' does not signify the time after trauma, as if

time proceeded in steps. In the post-traumatic city, the future has already arrived. The future emerges as the arena for a struggle over the present. Trauma, then, by clearing the field for a contest over the form of the future, amounts to a moment of potentiality through which the present might be reshaped.

In 'After the Event' (pages 50–7), Samantha Spurr explores the relationship between urbanism and conflict through a series of speculative and experimental design studios run in Beirut, Berlin and Shenzhen. If it is true that 'the future is an arena for a contest over the present', speculation comes to take on significant political force. Here, the speculative can no longer be considered a sort of play without consequences; rather it comes to be seen as the very space in which a contest over the present is fought.

Design experimentation and a broader sociopolitical agenda are only recently separated. Like an advance party with no army following, the ambition of the avant-garde and the messy reality of the world parted ways. Studios such as these in Beirut and the others like it gathered in this issue of ᗌ argue for their reconnection. They therefore all share the sense that the only way to renew the relevance of the profession is to redirect the energy and creativity of the avant-garde towards concrete problems. ᗌ

Notes
1. *I am reluctant to show you these terrors but I must.* Reluctance serves to mask the substantial libidinal investment we make in disaster itself so as to re-present it under the name of 'responsibility'. That is to say that we must appear as if we are only reluctantly calling on images of disaster and fear as a desperate call to change, to reform before it is too late. In this disavowed economy the ruin is the fetishistic example *par excellence* – antagonistically charged by desire and fear.
2. This reading is indebted to Mark Cousins' lecture series on 'The New' at the Architectural Association, London, in 1997.
3. Slavoj Žižek, *Welcome to the Desert of the Real*, Verso (London), 2002, p 44.

TRAUMA WITHIN THE WALLS
NOTES TOWARDS A PHILOSOPHY OF THE CITY

Renowned philosopher and critical theorist **Andrew Benjamin** provides a framework for thinking about trauma and the city. He returns to Sigmund Freud's definition of trauma as repressed memory and to Aeschylus' formulation of the unmasterable as portrayed in mythical Athens in the *Oresteia* trilogy. This view of unaccustomed or unpredictable forces, such as civic strife, as ever present and integral to democracy, enables the maintenance of the urban project avoiding repression.

Trauma does not come from the outside. Trauma is not to be understood as the consequence of invasion. And yet incursions from the outside and invasions are traumatic. Trauma involves a more complex sense of place. In psychoanalytic terms trauma is the reactivation of an occurrence that in the first instance was either simply absorbed or internalised. Despite what may have happened it remains unobserved and unnoticed. It is only with a subsequent occurrence that what was initially present becomes the site of investment. It is reworked and in being reworked acquires the status of symptom. For Freud this informs his analysis of the case of Emma in his 'Project for a Scientific Psychology'. While the detail of the case is not central, in this instance what matters is one of the conclusions Freud draws. Namely, that 'we invariably find that a memory is repressed which only becomes a trauma by deferred action (*die nur nachträlich zum Trauma geworden ist*).'[1] While the trauma is sexual in orientation, what matters in this context is that the trauma is produced. The response that is traumatic depends on the repression of an earlier occurrence. The event of trauma therefore is the relationship between these two particular occurrences. The event of trauma – an event holding itself apart from occurrences – has an original plurality.

The significance of the Freudian insight is twofold. In the first instance it demands undoing a conception of the traumatic that would have necessitated defining trauma purely in terms of an externality. What is reconfigured in the process is how the place of trauma is to be understood. The second involves another productive undoing. Rather than a strict opposition between the external and the internal there is an ineliminable and founding

Fadi Mansour, Re-Framing the City: A Monument of Radical Neutrality, AA Diploma Unit 6 (tutors: Chris Lee and Sam Jacoby), Architectural Association, London, 2009
Aerial view. Located on the old green line that divided east Beirut from west, this project conceives of the university campus as a type of infrastructure that encourages new forms of public occupation and cooperation through the participation of diverse stakeholders.

Simon Whittle, The Campus as Refuge, AA Diploma
Unit 6, Architectural Association, London, 2009
top: Polling station, Baghdad, 30 January 2006.
A single, highly militarised entrance to this Iraqi
election polling station creates single points of
vulnerability, and a high concentration of civilian
targets. Militarised zones cause extreme fragmentation
of the urban fabric; the primary symptom of this
fragmentation is the blast wall.

above: Future perimeter blast walls of main civil
institutions and the green zone, central Baghdad, 2006.
The defensive subdivision of the city into green
zones around institutions and red zones everywhere
else creates congested and heavily armed points of
engagement at the transition points between the two.
These become focal points of attacks and contain the
benefit these institutions provide to the surrounding city.

plurality. The setting contains that which while present, its mode of being present has inscribed within it the presence of a memory that has been repressed. There is thus a founding repression.

While Freud's immediate concern was providing an aetiology of the symptom that had to account for the place of the sexual within it, what is important here is not the forced relocation of the psychoanalytic into the city – as though the urban became a mere field of desires; rather what matters is the possibility of understanding the city and thus the urban field as having been, in part, constituted by repression and thus by a form of systematic forgetting. Within such a set-up, future occurrences – occurrences that may be the fact of invasion or acts of terror – rework what had hitherto been repressed and therefore allow for the presence of the traumatic. And yet, what was either forgotten or repressed can never simply just return. They cannot be recovered or remembered through an act of will. What this suggests is that, as a constituting condition, the city will always have contained that which falls beyond the work of memory, if memory is thought to complete. This setting entails that the city contain, as the continually unnamed, that which can be neither symbolised nor mastered. In sum, this means having to account not just for the presence of the unmasterable (the 'unmasterable' as the term identifying that refusal of symbolisation, unnameability and mastery's impossibility), but its role in the event of trauma.

Of the many formulations of the city that are bound up with the inscription of the unmasterable, one of the most significant occurs in Aeschylus' trilogy of tragedies, the *Oresteia*.[2] The setting is the following: the goddess Athena has, through an act which empowers the polis of Athens to become the locus of decision making, simultaneously undone both her own power and the rule of the gods. Athena brings about a 'catastrophe' (the word is the precise one used by the gods in the third play of the trilogy, *The Eumenides*

Of the many formulations of the city that are bound up with the inscription of the unmasterable, one of the most significant occurs in Aeschylus' trilogy of tragedies, the *Oresteia*.

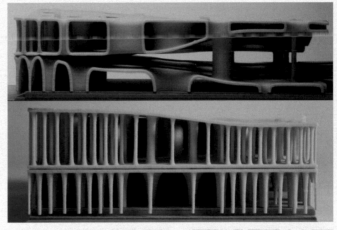

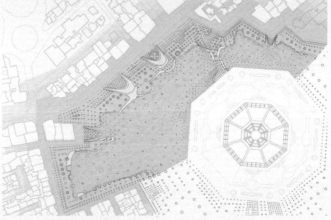

Simon Whittle, The Campus as Refuge,
AA Diploma Unit 6, Architectural Association, London, 2009
top: Project section. The project addresses the question: How does one reconcile the university's need for refuge and autonomy with providing a regenerative and beneficial proposal for the city? Taking the extreme situation in Baghdad, it rejects the current method of fortification and instead proposes an alternative form that draws from methods used to create privacy and security in the traditional Arabic fabric and modern force-protection guidelines to create a campus and city space that are both discrete entities yet closely interrelated. Rather than striking a purely defensive posture to the imposed and inherent conflict that occurs between the campus and the city, the proposal thus engages with the city, creating a space that not only fulfils the need for autonomy and security but also stimulates the community around it.

above: Ground-floor plan of the campus. The campus is inserted as an inhabitable wall into the set-back area around the Iraqi Supreme Court. The perimeter space of the building serves as market space for the surrounding city while the undulating slab provides a separated campus space for the university. Spaces vary from dense vaulted spaces at the front transitioning into inhabitable column spaces and then into a singular open space where the top level of columns thins out to become a roof structure with the column spaces becoming perforations for light.

490–1). However, this is not the 'catastrophe' of nihilism. It is an event that occasions. The response voiced by the Furies – voicing the position of the gods – is that while the democratic may have been enacted, democracy always brings with it that which will undo it. Democracy is attended by the continual threat of 'civil strife' (*stasis*). In sum, democracy will always have to negotiate with that which would disempower it. Such a possibility is always there within the structure of democracy. Eliminating it cannot take place therefore in the name of democracy. This possibility needs to be set against another more complex formulation made about the nature of the city. Here, the Chorus notes the following:

> There is a time when fear/the unaccustomed (*to deinon*) is good and ought to remain seated as a guardian of the heart. It is profitable to learn wisdom (*sophronein*) under the pressure of uncertainty.
> — *The Eumenides* 516–21

The significance of the passage depends upon how *to deinon* is understood. Rather than attempting to resolve that problem, as though there is a correct and definitive translation, what matters here is the possibility of attributing to it a double register. In the first instance when the term is uttered by the Chorus it corresponds to a sense of fear, a sense that brings with it its own conception of subjectivisation. The claim would be simply that fear generates reverence for Justice (*Dikè*). Moreover, in the lines that follow (521–6), the Chorus makes the claim that it does not matter if what is of concern is a 'single man' or a 'community of mortals'. In both instances

what is at stake is the 'same' (*omoiws*). From within this perspective a community of mortals is simply a plurality of singulars. It is not a generalised sense of commonality: provisionally being-in-common.[3] In other words, the identification of *to deinon* with fear is the project of the Chorus. The project both envisages and depends upon the singular individual (as a singularity or a plurality) as the subject of fear. While the reality of this position is not to be questioned, it is nonetheless possible to locate within the same lines another alternative. Not just an alternative interpretation, but one that is compatible with Athena's instantiation of the democratic.

The alternative necessitates allowing another register in these lines to predominate. In this instance it would involve emphasising the relationship that *to deinon* has to the work of wisdom (*sophronein*); wisdom as that which is acquired and deployed and as such is, *ab initio*, worldly. Within this setting *to deinon* can be understood as the response – and it may be fear – to that which is unaccustomed (*to deinon* would be the unaccustomed). However, it is not the unaccustomed that comes from an external source. Rather, the unaccustomed inhabits the city. It is the element that cannot be mastered but which demands constant engagement; an engagement guided by wisdom. It may be therefore that the 'unaccustomed' is *stasis* – the terms stage a similarity of concerns. However, it would not be *stasis* as the actuality of civil strife. Rather *stasis* would be the already present quality within democracy. *Stasis* names the necessity within the democratic – perhaps even as definitional of the democratic itself – of ineliminable forms of contestability. Democracy involves the recognition and affirmation of forms of powerlessness – the undoing of tyranny – and the repositioning of power. As such, of course, Athena becomes the exemplary figure of the democracy. Her abdication and her embracing the power of powerlessness is the catastrophe. She is not external to the creation of the democracy.

The unaccustomed is therefore not to be feared. Or rather it can only be feared if the link to wisdom has been severed. While the Chorus might want the connection between *to deinon* and *sophronein* to be maintained within

Fadi Mansour, Re-Framing the City: A Monument of Radical Neutrality,
AA Diploma Unit 6, Architectural Association, London, 2009
This project polemically reinterprets the Green Line in Beirut as a sectional void giving the possibility of a public infrastructure under the patronage of a Lebanese University that works twofold, in order to establish a new coexistence of the different urban factions. The Lebanese University, accessible to all communities, takes part in the marking of territories by monopolising the last remaining neutral ground and sustaining the void. The building is then made out of two elevated platforms with a public void in between. Structure and circulation are combined along the idea of the pinwheel, replacing the vertical shaft with a spiral, resulting in a pinwheel that works in 3-D. The two mirrored pinwheels shoot out in different directions and are superimposed in section as opposed to a planar adjacency. A taller narrower spiral fits within a shorter and wider one. Programme is placed in between the two at ground level. The spiral ends in a loop that acts as a transition between interior and exterior.

There cannot be a question of avoiding trauma. Trauma is the non-generalisable symptom. If it is possible to conceive of a traumatic urbanism, then the trauma will always need to be more than the infliction of violence.

an already determined framework, one in which *to deinon* entailed fear, it might be countered that as wisdom cannot have fear as its prompt, it is probably more accurate to locate the force of *to deinon* within the unaccustomed, thereby reinforcing the link to wisdom. The unaccustomed prompts thought. Fear would not. Wisdom, moreover, involves the endlessness of negotiation with that which cannot be mastered, namely the city as the locus of contestability. The unaccustomed becomes that which falls beyond the hold of predication and calculation. It would therefore be that which was allowed and equally that which allowed. There is, however, the other aspect of the unaccustomed (*to deinon*) and of *stasis*. Not only does *stasis* have a double register, integral to the creation of the democratic is the necessity that on the one hand it incorporate that which would undo it, while on the other there is the reciprocal necessity that the very unmasterability that leads to the incorporation of such an element generates that with which it becomes possible to judge, namely wisdom. There are two points concerning wisdom that need to be made in this context. The first is that it provides the means by which it is possible to engage and thus work with both contestability and the democratic's own internalised threat. The second is that wisdom, and thus its enactment as judgement, is not only sustained by the fabric of existence; the potentiality for its realisation forms a fundamental part of that fabric. Maintaining the presence of the unaccustomed opens a link to judgement and the democratic – a link, it should be added, that can be sustained to the extent that the unaccustomed retains the status of the unfamiliar. However, the unaccustomed is inherently precarious. There will always be the demand to turn the unfamiliar into the familiar. This is the point at which a return to Freud's conception of 'deferred action' becomes invaluable. The force of Freud's position was that it located the trauma within an act of constitution. An original state of affairs in being worked upon led to the emergence of the symptom. For Freud, what was at stake was giving an account of a traumatic state of affairs in terms of the transformation of that which had an original presence. In the strictly psychoanalytic context,

what this means is that an original event that was not perceived as sexual came to be positioned as such through its being reworked, and the process of reworking was integral to the production of the trauma. Hence traumas are produced.

The production presupposes transformation and a form of work on an original setting. In the case of the emergence of the democratic there is not an original setting in the same way. There is the presence of an original state of affairs comprising what has already been identified as the unmasterable; that is, what is maintained as the unaccustomed. Were it to be reworked, a process in which the unfamiliar and thus the unaccustomed would be subject to a series of attempted transformations in which familiarity and the accustomed would be the end result, then it would be possible to account for such attempts in terms of trauma. Trauma becomes the appropriate term precisely because the movement to familiarity – a movement which involves imposition and the symbolic levelling of points of contestation and negotiation (a symbolism that can, of course, become literal) – will be accompanied by the attempted transformation of an element whose transformation will be its ruination. That element is the unaccustomed. Moreover, what also runs the risk of ruination is the relationship between the unaccustomed and wisdom. What would be ruined is that which obtained originally, namely the interplay of the unaccustomed and commonality. Trauma in both instances is an act of transformation. Within the strictly psychoanalytic model, what is reworked and the process of reworking are themselves the work of an economic set of relations between the conscious and the unconscious. There cannot be a question of avoiding trauma. Trauma is the non-generalisable symptom. If it is possible to conceive of a traumatic urbanism, then the trauma will always need to be more than the infliction of violence. Trauma becomes an infliction that tries to rid an original set-up of the unmasterability that defines it. The symptom here would be different. Its location would be within the continual attempt to name and thus control the unaccustomed. The unaccustomed locates at the centre of the city a founding sense of estrangement. Negotiating with forms of original estrangement means having to abandon the project of mastery. This abandonment has implications as much within the realm of planning as it does within politics. Recognising that the unaccustomed is an always already-present quality within the urban means that integral to the urban project is maintaining it. Trauma emerges when that element is reworked in the name of either the similar or the universal. Hence what is needed is another form of deferred action. The form in which the original setting is both reworked and maintained. ⍗

Notes

1. Sigmund Freud, 'Project for a Scientific Psychology', in *The Complete Psychological Works of Sigmund Freud*, Vol 1, trans James Strachey, The Hogarth Press (London), 1966, p 356. (German edition: Sigmund Freud, *Aus den Anfängen der Psychoanalyse*, Imago Publishing (London), 1950, (p 435.)
2. References to the *Oresteia* are to the Loeb Classical Library Edition. Aeschylus, *Oresteia*, trans Alan H Sommerstein, Harvard University Press (Cambridge, MA), 2008. (Translations have been modified on occasions.)
3. This term is discussed in much greater detail and its place within ancient Greek philosophy more firmly established in Andrew Benjamin, *Place, Commonality and Judgment: Continental Philosophy and the Ancient Greeks*, Continuum Books (London), November 2010.

Fadi Mansour, Re-Framing the City: A Monument of Radical Neutrality, AA Diploma Unit 6, Architectural Association, London, 2009
Longitudinal section. As opposed to framing a dislocated space of refuge, the proposal frames the existing urban fabric. Architecture itself is the frame: an open campus that holds public spaces. The academic institution takes part in the marking of territories by monopolising the last remaining neutral ground.

THE SPACE-TIME OF PRE-EMPTION
AN INTERVIEW WITH BRIAN MASSUMI

The philosopher **Brian Massumi** is known for his explorations of experience, art, media theory and politics and has recently turned his attention to understanding the impact that sustained fear has on perception in a post-9/11 world. In an interview with guest-editor **Charles Rice**, Massumi defines threat by distinguishing it from real danger and how it manifests itself in both civil and military spaces of pre-emptive action that are primed to the possibilities of attack.

inset: Philosopher Brian Massumi's recent work has sought to come to terms with the theoretical structure of pre-emption so that we may better understand what action – political, social, architectural – might currently mean.

Anish Kapoor, Cloud Gate, Chicago, 2006
'Affect is an action word. It has as much to do with action-potential as feeling tone, and the felt field of potential action is environmental, which is to say immediately collective.' Internal reflections in Anish Kapoor's Cloud Gate sculpture show what Massumi calls 'a space of collective reindividuation', one where bodies 'react differently together' to the affective environment.

If the often-cited 'recent events' of the post-9/11 age indicate anything, it is that danger is no longer 'clear and present'. Rather, an indistinct though ever-present fog of threat permeates the space of everyday life. Within this fog – for there is no without – reaction to what clearly appears has been supplanted by pre-emption in relation to what is yet to come. Recently, philosopher Brian Massumi has been thinking through this foggy new reality, trying to come to terms with the theoretical structure of pre-emption so that we may better understand what action – political, social, architectural – might mean currently.[1]

Massumi's first move is to theorise threat by distinguishing its nature from danger. Threat possesses a different time signature: 'Danger lurks. It is ready and waiting, already constituted. This makes it discriminable in principle. The trick is making the discrimination, seeing the lurking for what it is, and responding to it proportionately. The way that threat presents is very different. In today's complex "threat environment", threat is ever present but never clearly present. There is an essential element of indeterminacy to it. It doesn't lurk; it looms, vaguely, unplaceably. So that even if you sense it coming, it still always comes as a surprise. Danger lurks into the present from a past chain of causes, which is in principle definable as the danger becomes discriminable. Threat looms from the future, where surprises come from. It is felt more in the key of futurity, as a something pressing whose nature is yet to be defined, and may never be defined. A threat is a present sign of a future event that may or may not come to pass. When it does, it comes on an off-note. The fact that it was already looming doesn't prevent the particular form it ends up taking from striking with a senselessness equal to the surprise. The different relationship to time creates a different affective tone – the already feared unforeseen – as well as a different pragmatic posture towards threat. Given its indeterminate nature, there can be no proportionate response to it.'[2]

The posture entailed by threat is that of pre-emption: 'Pre-emption is the attempt to deal politically, militarily or in the civil sphere with a danger which has not yet fully emerged, that is, a threat.' This quality of threat as what has not yet fully emerged brings with it a particular spatial dimension. For Massumi, this space is environmental; to engage with threat is to engage with what is not yet separate from the background. Pre-emption thus brings with it a kind of environmental awareness that also contains a pragmatic posture of preparation for what is yet to happen. The space of pre-emption, however, is not a place. Rather, it emerges from a vague field of potential action, and it does not necessarily correspond to functional divisions of spaces that might already be in place. To explain this, Massumi refers to Eyal Weizman's account in his book *Hollow Land* of the way in which Israeli military forces have enacted spaces of operation by literally blasting passages through the private, interior space of an urban area in order to outflank an enemy occupying the more 'conventional' exterior territory of streets, squares and vantage points:[3]

'There is the translation of an existing space into an operative space defined less by a configuration of positions than by qualities of potential movement. By that I mean that it is defined by ability to irrupt unexpectedly, to break out of or to break into the existing spatial grid, anywhere, at any moment. This irruptive potential enables a completely new and different pattern of movement that is not on the grid, but flows through it following different principles of circulation, and implying a different repertory of tactics. That difference in dynamic patterning is what I call the operative space of pre-emptive action. What is pre-empted here is the battle of positions, and the traditional form of the siege or occupation of an existing lay of the land. The important points are, first, that the space is emergent, and its emergence is enactive – it is created in and through its performance – and second, that the leading edge of its emergence is time-based: surprise. It is still a question of spatial design, broadly speaking, because this pre-emptive space of operation is produced through a very particular spatial technique: burrowing through walls. What is so particular about this is that strategy addresses the production of space through the dimension of time. It meets threat on its own proto-territory.'

opposite: 'If the often-cited "recent events" of the post-9/11 age indicate anything, it is that danger is no longer "clear and present".' Air-testing units hang inside boxes as scientists release a colourless, odourless and harmless 'tracer gas' in a drill to see how to respond to a chemical or biological attack in New York, 8 August 2005. The US Department of Homeland Security funded the test which lasted six days, allowing scientists to model airflow to aid emergency responders.

Zoriah Miller, War Photography, Gaza, 2006
below: An apartment complex severely damaged during fighting in the Gaza Strip, 28 April 2006, exemplifying the Israeli Defence Force strategy of moving through walls. 'There is the translation of an existing space into an operative space defined less by a configuration of positions than by qualities of potential movement.'

Massumi suggests that this conceptual logic can be applied to civil spaces 'to the extent that they become saturated with security and surveillance mechanisms, aimed at surprising a surprise in the making, before it has fully emerged. The watchword is "anomalous behaviour detection", with a tactical repertory of "rapid response" capabilities poised to trigger into operation an emergent space of pre-emptive action that beats danger to the mark, besting it at its own threatening game. At this "soft" end of the spectrum of pre-emptive action, the space of urban life is transformed into the civil society equivalent of the military proto-territory we just discussed. Public space is saturated with threat and counter-threat, tensed with watching and waiting, poised for danger, perpetually on edge. This creates a very different kind of urban ambience.'

This ambience belongs to perception, a bodily feeling organised environmentally before cognitive apprehension, and which is primed or preconditioned by the space of possible action. There is a question of design here in the extent to which the space of pre-emption is arranged according to techniques and technologies that will come into play in the operative moment of reaction; however, the design is spatial to the extent that these techniques and technologies are not simply innocent elements, dormant before they are called upon. The priming or saturation of spaces in advance of the events perpetually to unfold is not separate from that 'environmental' unfolding: 'Perhaps the oddest property of pre-emption is that it produces what it fights. What effectively makes the urban space an on-all-the-time threat environment is the ubiquity of the security responses embedded in it. The ambience this produces is one of insecurity. After all, security only makes sense under conditions of insecurity. Securing presupposes insecurity. The deployment of security measures implants that presupposition throughout the space in

The Chicago (Tze'elim base) urban warfare training site in the Negev desert, southern Israel, 2005. Precast holes in walls literally concretise the proto-space of battle as a training simulation.

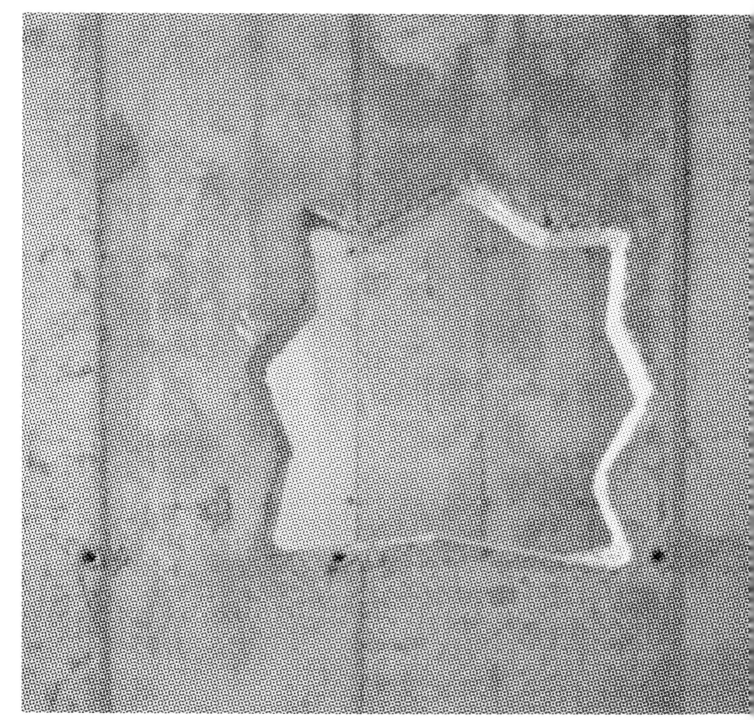

> The perception-event of threat's perpetual unfolding in space is an individuating experience for bodies poised on the cusp of action. It is an experience that differentiates rather than unifies feeling-bodies becoming acting- and reacting-subjects because the histories and dispositions of each individual will yield a unique response.

which they are embedded. Security produces its own conditions. It pre-emptively produces the threat environment it responds to – and needs to justify itself. It is actually the signs of security strategically distributed throughout public space – the ever-present video surveillance cameras, for example – that most effectively bring threat from its looming future into the space of the present. This is a crucial consideration for architectural and urban design. Hiding the signs might only intensify the effect by making them even more menacingly looming.'

The perception-event of threat's perpetual unfolding in space is an individuating experience for bodies poised on the cusp of action. It is an experience that differentiates rather than unifies feeling-bodies becoming acting- and reacting-subjects because the histories and dispositions of each individual will yield a unique response. The environment, from this point of view, is structured as a kind of superposition of different paths of unfolding: 'It is important to keep in mind that the "ambience", the affect of pre-emption, is not subjective in the sense of being limited to an internal state of an individual. Affect is an action word. It has as much to do with action-potential as feeling tone, and the felt field of potential action is environmental, which is to say immediately collective. Bodies react differently together, and that redefines what the environment is for each, and what each is for the environment. The operative space they cohabit is a space of collective re-individuation.'

Rather than see pre-emption as an all-encompassing spatialisation of threat in a negative and oppressive dynamic of authoritarian power, the body, and its related practices of action poised on the cusp of potential can be seen from this inventive angle of collective re-individuation. 'What,' asks Massumi, 'would it mean to design for that? Can spatial design extract that potential from pre-emption and embed it in an otherwise inflected affective environment?'

The modulation and inflection of a dynamic field through differential actions are by now well-understood concepts within architectural design, not least because of Massumi's own work in making these concepts available to architecture during the last two decades.[4] If, in the emergence of the threat-environment, anything has changed with regard to architecture's understanding of the urban as a dynamic field, it is that the flows and dynamics that might drive the inflections of design are not to be taken as innocent or neutral material, though they may initially be abstract and without determined outcome. They are now part of the murky, indistinct presence-without-appearance of threat that owes its cultural purchase to a priming through the media environment. This priming is particular. It is a priming, suggests Massumi, 'for distrust, for the avoidance of encounters, for a cringing posture to the unexpected'. Since this effectively modulates a field of potential action, Massumi refers to the 'affective effectiveness of the media'. In short, the 'unprogrammed', the 'chance encounter', the 'interstitial', concepts so central to architectural strategies of the last 20 years, are now construed as threatening, as their images are turned towards the future of their vague but inevitable actualization of a threat environment. Yet 'the performative', the 'actualisation of potential' and 'collective re-individuation' are also part of the logic of an unfolding of a space of operation whose outcome is not determined in advance. If architecture is to do more than concretise uncertainty in the present, and thereby memorialise threat over time, then its own media environment must become 'affectively effective' in a renewed way. ⌀

Notes
1. See Brian Massumi, 'Perception Attack: The Force to Own Time', in Jane Elliot and Derek Attridge (eds), *Theory After 'Theory'*, Routledge (London), 2010; Massumi, 'The Future Birth of the Affective Fact: The Political Ontology of Threat', in Greg Seigworth and Melissa Greg (eds), *The Affect Reader*, Duke University Press (Durham), forthcoming; Massumi, 'National Enterprise Emergency: Steps Toward an Ecology of Powers', *Theory, Culture & Society*, Vol 26, No 6, 2009, pp 153–85; and Massumi, 'Potential Politics and the Primacy of Pre-emption', *Theory & Event*, Vol 10, No 2, 2007, 34 paras.
2. Interview with Brian Massumi at Cornell University, 17 February 2010. All quotations from Massumi are from this interview.
3. See Eyal Weizman, *Hollow Land: Israel's Architecture of Occupation*, Verso (London), 2007, pp 185–219.
4. See especially Brian Massumi, *Parables for the Virtual: Movement, Affect, Sensation*, Duke University Press (Durham), 2003; Massumi, 'Strange Horizon: Buildings, Biograms and the Body Topologic', ⌀ *Hypersurface Architecture*, Vol 69, Nos 9–10, 1999, pp 12–19; Massumi, 'Sensing the Virtual, Building the Insensible', ⌀ *Hypersurface Architecture*, Vol 68, Nos 5–6, 1998, pp 16–25; and Massumi, 'The Diagram as Technique of Existence', *Any*, No 23, 1998, pp 42–7.

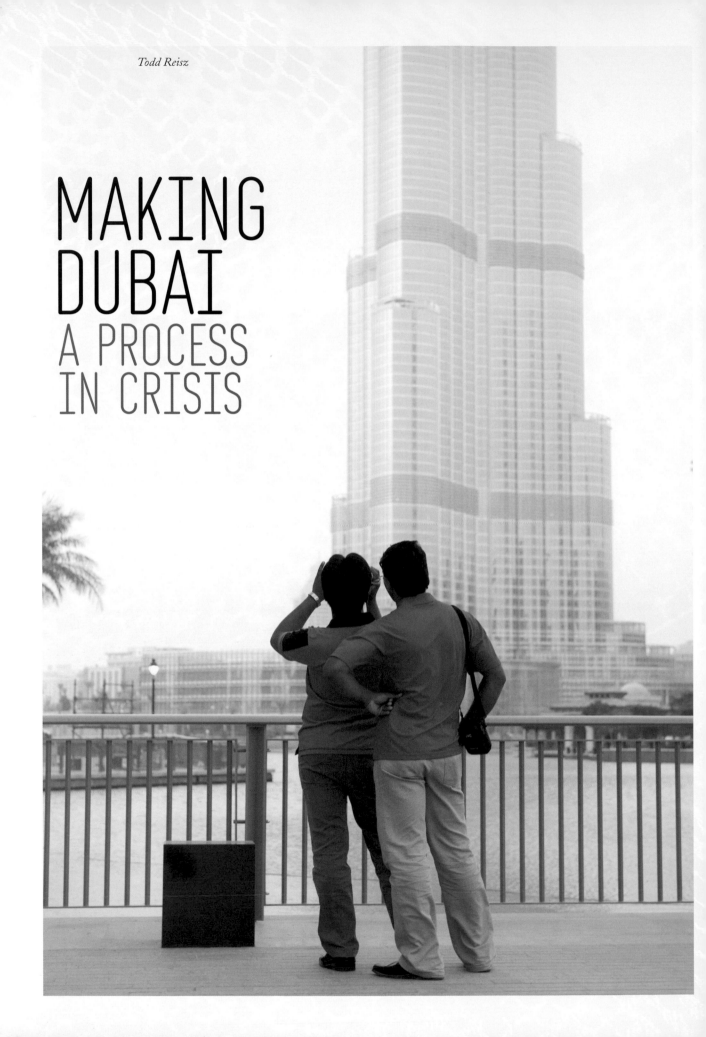

Todd Reisz

MAKING DUBAI
A PROCESS IN CRISIS

The world financial crisis of 2009 brought the onward march of property development in Dubai to a standstill. **Todd Reisz** describes how the city's PR community responded to the predicament with a cathartic call for honesty and transparency. Reisz, however, questions the consultants' understanding of the Dubai Dream, which though built out of no more than images, is also constructed out of the hopes of the Arab world.

On 20 October 2009, a luncheon entitled 'Restoring Trust – The Challenge of Exiting the Downturn' was held at Dubai's Capital Club and focused on a complicated but familiar triangle: Dubai, the crisis and the public relations response. The speakers were two of the city's celebrated public relations strategists, Dave Robinson and Eileen Wallis, and around 50 people also concerned with Dubai and its future filled the dining room of the local business club to hear the story from their corner. While the guests were still finishing their desserts, one woman who worked for a well-known consultancy firm as a reputation management consultant, a 'growing niche market', according to her, not to be confused with crisis management consulting, was asked how she was surviving the crisis. Her reply was that it was difficult giving reputation advice because, well, it wasn't being taken. And things were getting worse.

She was right that things were getting worse. By October, there was already a pile-up of disquieting circumstances: sinking real-estate prices, stalled development projects, departing expatriates and increasing hyperboles in the press. Worse was still to come. In November, Dubai World, one of Dubai's three important holding companies, would admit its inability to handle near to $60 billion in debt burden.

More than a month before Dubai World's unravelling, Robinson, Wallis and their audience were all pushing a wholesale solution to Dubai's woes over their lunch crumbs: Dubai needed a press relations strategy, one that was prepared to tell the truth. Honesty, it was said many times, was the only way. With all the head shaking and communal chastising towards Dubai, I began to wonder why there wasn't also

any self-congratulating. Dubai *was* PR strategy; it was a constant crafting of words and images to project a Dubai that did not yet exist. It was so good, so strong, that it meant few had to take into consideration what was actually happening on the ground.

This was a whole new generation of PR experts sitting at this lunch. They had likely arrived too late to aid in master developer Nakheel's meteoric rise as a global name without a portfolio to sustain it, in the establishment of a Dubai bourse before there was a banking community to support one, in the reinvention of DP World after the American fiasco, in the Burj al Arab becoming one of the world's most recognisable buildings. But still, those seated at lunch represented the legacy of delivering truths before they were fully woven. They were also part of a city that didn't yet exist. But it seemed now was the time of reckoning: Dubai's government and its companies needed to listen to the PR experts, but for new reasons.

For the months leading up to October, there had been a clampdown on Dubai companies' relationships with the press. Few were talking. Like children who had been kept too long from the playing fields, the assembly was cracking from the pressure. There needed to be more transparency: Dubai needed to talk to the world, PR people needed to be able to do their jobs. Calls for 'transparency' gave way to calls for 'embrace'. Towards the end of the group cheer, the topic had turned to 'all the bad press' – the images of a sinking Dubai, the Darth Vader and Mickey Mouse references and so on by Western journalists coming in for a day or two and leaving with damning but entertaining articles about the city. How must Dubai approach these arriving journalists? Wallis felt compelled

Rather than in the city itself, Dubai's crisis is rooted in a financial rumpus and the PR strategy that fuelled it: the prosperous pursuit of inordinate amounts of capital from the world's most respectable banks with nothing more than an orchestra of words and images.

to answer: 'You need to embrace them. E m b r a c e them. E m b r a c e them. E m b r a c e them.' After each time she said 'Embrace them', she halfway lifted herself out of her seat and body-gestured a terrific air-bearhug and then fell back in her seat again.

As the rest of the group watched Wallis regain her composure, the head of a local bank, maybe the only Emirati in the room, took the microphone. He retorted: 'We have tried that before. It doesn't work,' and put the microphone on the table with a sonic thud.

The last year and a half of crisis in Dubai has unleashed a cascade of *Schadenfreude*. Crisis was for many critics vindication, a fateful sign that they had been right all along about the city: that Dubai was a failed attempt at making one.

Those critics have missed the point. Dubai's crisis is not about urbanism or architecture. No model of development, or as some would say the lack thereof, has been proven a failure. If there ever was a model, it is still being pursued, in Dubai and in other Gulf cities whose deep coffers of petrodollars have given them elasticity during the crisis (look at Doha, Riyadh and Abu Dhabi). The most successful designers of Dubai – be they architects, planners, engineers, artists, management consultants, bankers or entrepreneurs – are still designing, either in Dubai or, more potently, somewhere else nearby.

The critcs' poetic deployment of 'ghost town' imagery only gives the city's champions an easier means of responding. By focusing their comebacks on the city's physical components, Dubai's leaders can avoid providing answers on the topics where the city is most bankrupt. In the process, Dubai has appropriated the critic's trump card: time. Empty buildings will eventually be filled; the metro is working to connect once isolated islands of development; the city is becoming a place of the normal. Faster than it came, Dubai's whirlwind pace has lost its gusto. When in earlier days time had to be beaten, it now just has to be endured.

opposite: Progress and promises at the Business Bay commercial, residential and business complex, Dubai: stalled tower construction behind advertising for The Villa development project. Described by its developers as a 'new city within a city', Business Bay suffered delays even before the onset of the global crisis. Its construction site is protected by signs for developments elsewhere which might never be realised, or at least will be pursued on much lengthier timelines.

bottom: A billboard for Business Bay along Sheikh Zayed Road. The $30 billion development project has not yet extended its 2015 opening date, but its number of towers has been decreased from 260 to 240. During 2009 and early 2010, work on most towers all but stopped. The first tower opened in early 2010.

below: Business Bay's Executive Towers complex is made up of 12 towers designed by WS Atkins. Constantly beset by opening delays, its 2,150 new residences have only added weight to Dubai's housing surplus.

below: Electrical towers in front of Dubai Marina and the Jumeirah Lake Towers residential and office complex. Both of these projects, and the electricity plants built and proposed to light them, now represent the surplus in built housing (fuelled by speculative investors). Some property analysts predict that Dubai will suffer from a housing oversupply for the next 10 years.

bottom: Dubai Marina and Sheikh Zayed Road seen from the metro on the first day of its opening to the public. Dubai Marina is approximately 25 kilometres (15.5 miles) from Burj Khalifa, a trip that can take an hour in traffic, or just 15 minutes by metro.

opposite left: On 10 September 2009, the metro opened to everyday residents of Dubai. It was a day-long celebration of new rituals in the city. Residents boarded the trains and saw the city from a perspective not yet experienced before the metro's opening.

opposite right: Leading up to the opening of the metro, concerns were voiced that it would instigate awkward social interactions. Instead, riders have described how Dubai residents are finding new ways of interacting across economical and social lines. One commentator has described the metro as Dubai's first public realm.

Rather than in the city itself, Dubai's crisis is rooted in a financial rumpus and the PR strategy that fuelled it: the prosperous pursuit of inordinate amounts of capital from the world's most respectable banks with nothing more than an orchestra of words and images. To secure the over-leveraged funds, the present was merely an ersatz for tomorrow. PR had created this truth and the banks had bought it, but now PR's acolytes were asking the mechanism to come clean, to pull aside the very arras PR had helped construct.

The fake catharsis over lunch will not ever result in a true exposure of Dubai's losses; it is doubtful anyone would want that. Dubai has admitted some fault and therefore has exposed some vulnerability. Admission of fault has also revealed how a wounded giant can attract sympathy. The *Financial Times*, for instance, ran a story on 8 April 2009 about how Dubai 'feels' friendlier, abandoning its usual focus on numbers to describe a 'more liveable place'.[1]

The *Financial Times*' soft spot for Dubai would be short-lived. For the first time in a year when numbers were constantly sinking deeper in the red, Dubai World's November announcement signalled the first true expressions of fear for Dubai's future from international bankers, but without an ounce of self-criticism. It took Prince Alwaleed of Saudi Arabia, the single person who lost the most in Wall Street's fumbles, to expose the contrived surprise and puppy-dog whining of Western bankers at Dubai World's proposed standstill: they should have known all along that these companies and Dubai's strategies were never less than opaque. Dubai's greatest loss is that it should never expect such wilful naivety again. Good riddance, according to all parties.

This is not Dubai's first crisis. It certainly will not be its last. It is a city surrounded by crisis (see Yemen, Pakistan), defined by crisis (its constant need to make something from nothing), and even profiting from crisis (see Iran). Dubai, its champions are quick to say, is the big hope of the Arab world. It offers peace and stability, a chance at wealth, smooth highways and a clean, blackout-free existence. It is now a cliché to mention that children in Algeria proudly don Dubai T-shirts depicting skylines and camels.

The blows Dubai took in 2009 have lifted places like Doha and Abu Dhabi as more assured investment opportunities, but Dubai still reigns in the imaginations of millions of people between North Africa and Southeast Asia. A Pakistani might take a chauffeur job in Doha, but he would much rather take the same job in Dubai. Similarly, a Syrian, after being laid off in Dubai, will hold out as long as possible before he takes a job in Doha. No matter how many derisive labels one side of the world conjures up for Dubai, the city still stands for freedom, daresay hope, in a part of the world whose population (and growth rate) easily outstrips that of North America and the European Union. Dubai's greatest export and perhaps its last chance at survival lie in this image. And it is one that no PR agent could ever take credit for.

As Dubai still holds sway in a vast region as much misunderstood as it can be, the city also searches for a new posture. The recent openings of two megaprojects, the Burj Khalifa and the Dubai Metro, both represent a more human Dubai. That was not their original intention – when was a world's tallest tower a humanist project? But Dubai is now a city that knows the story of Babel and the value of a metro ride that from an elevated rail displays a functioning city gradually emerging, one healing its growth wounds and tempering its bravado so that it might one day have another chance at being great. ⌂

Note
1. Roula Khalaf, 'Don't Rule Out Dubai Comeback', *Financial Times*, 8 April 2009.

Anthony Acciavatti

CHANGES OF STATE

SLOW-MOTION TRAUMA IN THE GANGETIC PLAINS OF INDIA

In recent years, the vicissitudes wrought by harsh weather patterns and natural disasters have resulted in hurricanes and earthquakes and had a catastrophic impact on people's lives. The Ganges River Corridor in northern India is a region that perennially undergoes extreme changes in weather and climate with the onslaught of the monsoon season. **Anthony Acciavatti**, in his Dynamic Atlas series of drawings, has measured the effects of rainfall and agrarian processes in relation to the fast-paced modes of urbanisation in the area.

Anthony Acciavatti, Dynamic
Atlas, India Ganges, 2007
The super-surface refers to the
extraordinary variety of hydrological
infrastructure composing the state
of Uttar Pradesh. Large-scale
canals, barrages and shallow
pumping mechanisms litter the
state to create a highly engineered,
if uncoordinated, surface.

FORMATION OF SUPER SURFACE

NON-CULTIVATED LAND

IRRIGATED AREA
(x 100,000 ha)

PRE-PLAN (BEFORE 1950)
25.53

FIRST PLAN (1951-56)
28.83

FOURTH PLAN (1969-74)
40.80

SEVENTH PLAN (1975-80)
66.58

ANNUAL PLAN (1997-98)
71.12

ANNUAL PLAN (1997-98)
71.12

IRRIGATED AREA (x 100,000 ha)	
PRE PLAN (BEFORE 1950)	25.53
FIRST PLAN (1951-56)	28.83
FOURTH PLAN (1969-74)	40.80
SEVENTH PLAN (1985-90)	66.58
ANNUAL PLAN (1997-98)	71.12

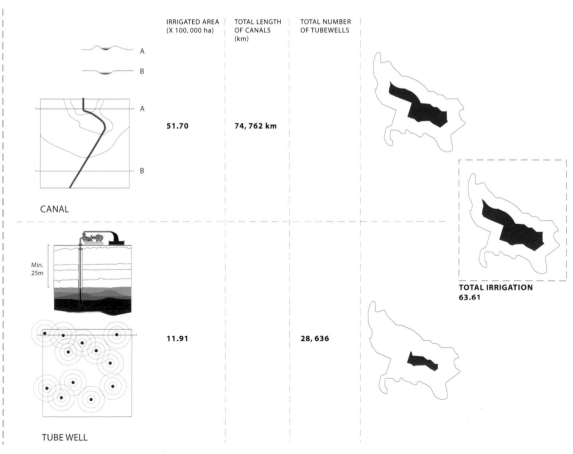

	IRRIGATED AREA (X 100,000 ha)	TOTAL LENGTH OF CANALS (km)	TOTAL NUMBER OF TUBEWELLS	
CANAL	51.70	74,762 km		
TUBE WELL	11.91		28,636	

TOTAL IRRIGATION
63.61

Min.
25m

A
B

A

B

45

Beyond the dense urbanism of a city like Mumbai or the IT centres of Bangalore and Hyderabad lies the Ganges river corridor in the state of Uttar Pradesh. Though the immense territory appears outside the image of modern India, for the past 150 years this 'cow belt' has been situated at the very centre of a struggle to establish a productive countryside with its affiliated infrastructures of canals, barrages and roadways. Rather than a collision of 'countryside versus city', political and material conflicts arise over a shared set of support structures.

The seat of former empires, principalities and satrapies, the Ganges river corridor presents a fertile meeting of religious and cultural heritage, agricultural cultivation and diffuse forms of urbanisation supported by an elaborate network of hydrological and transportation infrastructures. The extreme changes in weather and climate caused by the onslaught of the wet monsoon (late June through late August) transforms the region from an arid and parched condition to a wet and gelatinous one. For this reason, it is a territory whose urbanisation was culturally and ideologically bound by these seasonal rains. As the seasonal and mechanical distribution of water are so intertwined with maintaining life and staving off famine and civil unrest, this condition asks questions of architecture and urbanism across a variety of scales. Today, settlement has expanded by means of modern forms of artificial irrigation like canals, tube-wells and miniature hand-held pumping mechanisms. The corridor has been conceived and constructed as a highly calibrated 'super-surface'[1] of hydrological infrastructure, siphoning water from the Ganges and Yamuna rivers as well as from natural aquifers, all to support everything from high-intensity

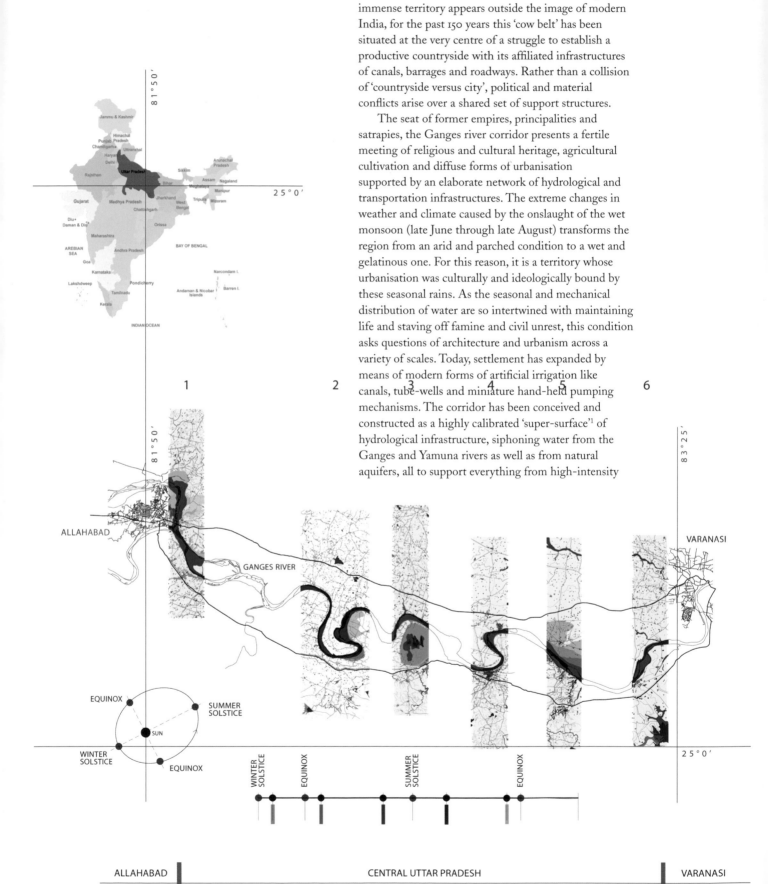

ALLAHABAD	CENTRAL UTTAR PRADESH	VARANASI
COMPACT CITY	OPEN TERRITORY	COMPACT CITY

cash crops such as sugar cane and industrial processing to the domestic needs of nearly 200 million people.

The region is host to one of the oldest and largest bureaucracies of water management in the world. It is entrusted with not only distributing water, but also with indirectly managing urban growth, and has imposed a highly convoluted public works system that encourages diffuse forms of urbanisation and unrestrained resource extraction practices. Despite this, physical planning and government policy have traditionally hinged on an urban–rural divide in terms of the consolidated city versus open territory. Within this model of development, the traditional consolidated city is characterised by controlled density and well-defined blocks and plazas. On the other hand, open territory epitomises pastoral, agricultural lands. As a model for growth, these ideas still resonate within the bureaucracies of India, even though they have no operative agency.

The belief in technology to deliver a more economically productive future has directed imaginations of India's progress for the past several hundred years, from the occupation by the British East India Company to the modern nation-state. Following independence in 1947 and the planned economic growth of the successive Soviet-inspired Five Year Plans, India embarked on monumental rural infrastructural development through the extension of canals and roadways. By the 1960s decentralised forms of irrigation like tube-wells and portable water-pumping mechanisms were coupled with genetically modified seeds to support the Green Revolution. Today, with nearly one-sixth of India's billion-plus

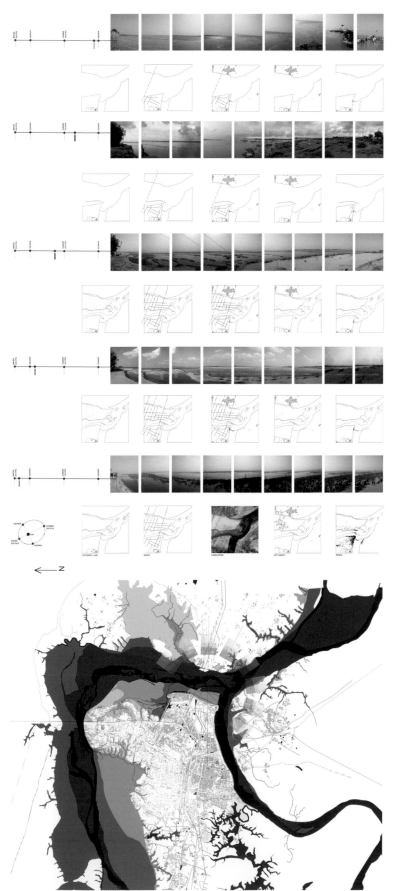

Anthony Acciavatti, Dynamic Atlas, India Ganges, 2007
opposite: The traditional compact city versus open territory still informs development practices in northern India. However infrastructural innovation and a rapidly growing population have dissolved the differences between both models.

Anthony Acciavatti, Dynamic Atlas, India Ganges, 2006
left: Located at the confluence of the Ganges, Yamuna and mythical Saraswati rivers, each year during the month of Magh (January/February) the Triveni Sangam transforms from a series of islands into a temporary city. The drawing uses a single solar cycle to map the coincidence of celestial and terrestrial forces.

population living in Uttar Pradesh, and liberalisation of the national economy, an urban agro-polis has emerged across the Gangetic plains. This new urban–rural hybrid comprises patchy and dispersed urban settlement, stressing elemental resources like water and food as well as arable land.

While most modes of trauma, such as hurricanes, tornados or earthquakes, are instant and happen in a snapshot of a few days or weeks, these dispersed forms of urbanisation create a natural disaster in slow motion. A monsoon-fed productive countryside relies on the cultivation of a thin and expansive surface and produces fundamentally transient forms of space largely shaped by the distribution and absorption rates of water. Today more than ever water is not channellised and absorbed by the natural topography and ground cover, but is diverted across paved surfaces, concrete roofs and agricultural fields.

The changes wrought by this new pattern can only be perceived through measured drawings, rendering the role of the architect and the urbanist essential within this new and diffuse landscape. Traditional methods of cartography and representation, which largely rely on fixed objects and topographic difference in terms of contours, fail to commensurate the trans-scalar geometries and shapes of rapid urbanisation with the dynamics of material composition understood in terms of hard and soft, wet and dry.

Due to the nature of this unusual urban-agrarian-riparian composition, it is important to rethink and represent the changes of state this territory has undergone within two distinct yet interrelated spheres: the abundance and scarcity of water produced by the annual wet monsoon, and the species of infrastructure used to capture and harvest the deluge produced by it. In this way, the Ganges river corridor is at once a densely populated river belt and occupies a number of soluble states (water, mud, dirt, dust, deity and atmosphere). The term 'state' here is used to refer to the coincidence of physical changes of state (molecular transformations from solid to liquid to gas), but also political and cultural changes of state (the village, the town, the city, the nation as well as the religious festival and winter and spring harvests). In other words, the impact of weather and climate are intertwined in the matrix of everyday life in all of its manifestations. The capriciousness of rainfall and the rigid infrastructures put in place to redistribute water affirm a perennial trauma of too little or too much water, and subsequent post-traumatic relationships caused by an inability to correlate cause and effect, revealing the scales and forms of urbanisation across this vast plain. The compelling need to adapt or to disintegrate, historically, to the drastic changes of the Gangetic plains made climatic responsiveness the commanding theme of human settlement along this unmatched waterway. With the exponential growth in human populations and the widespread use of canals and water pumps to manipulate the effects of climate, modifying climate ranges from the scale of the single-family dwelling to the larger territory, in effect promoting a territorial reverse engineering.

The relationships across material and cultural patterns offer the opportunity to better frame environmental change and typological permutations of settlement across this animate topos.

Anthony Acciavatti, Dynamic Atlas, India Ganges, 2007
The effects of subsurface water infrastructures like shallow mechanised wells have encouraged diffuse forms of urbanism, dramatically fracturing the edges of cities and countryside alike.

Dynamic Atlas

Official representations of the territory rarely capture the rhythmic interplay between the states of ground and water. Instead, they often settle on static, cartographic imagery or data sets with no spatial surrogate. Maps are needed in order to take advantage of the unique meteorological, environmental and urbanistic opportunities presented by the Ganges river corridor. The relationships across material and cultural patterns offer the opportunity to better frame environmental change and typological permutations of settlement across this animate topos. In principle, designing buildings and designing territory for development (extending infrastructural and economic fabric across the hinterlands), in this context, should be more integrated to address the unique scales and pressures shaping the region. The growing scarcity of fresh water and available land has necessitated a demand for better-operating urbanisation models in relationship to the dynamics of the Gangetic plains. The redundant expansion of individual and government-sponsored hydrological infrastructures for domestic and industrial use make it imperative to investigate and speculate on the transformative potential of water infrastructure to generate urban form. Hydrotechnologies and their concomitant programmes are at once physical and political enterprises that can bridge the uncoordinated extraction of water and the need to adequately replenish aquifers and rivers. Only through reconsidering the different dimensions of these urban generators can we begin to adequately hallucinate on alternative settlement configurations and methods of growth.

The Dynamic Atlas is a cartographic set of drawings that combine different scales of information and time on a single picture plane. The drawings use the annual solar and lunar cycles as a datum to measure the effects of rainfall and agrarian processes in relation to the fast-paced modes of urbanisation within the Ganges river corridor. The atlas engages the variables of water within this territory as an unexplored frontier within the making of urbanism and urbanity. If ground – as simultaneously a modern 'development' imperative and a locus of unbroken religio-cultural tradition thousands of years old – continues to inhabit a cartographic no-man's-land, it will neither encourage doubt nor avidity about how it actually affirms and sustains itself across this vast alluvial corridor.

In order to move beyond the spectacle trauma of a single news cycle, drawings must lucidly engage the lunacy of weather and cultural mores fuelling urbanism. Only through a critical reading of the disparate processes that have shaped this territory – from field and pasture to city to agro-polis – can we retrace the larger motivations that have reformatted this ground in order to project an underlying infrastructural framework for alternative futures. Representation must play a critical role as both a body of knowledge arrived at through methodical study as well as a technical tool to direct growth. In doing so we can better picture the veiled ecological and infrastructural pressures that have encouraged diffuse urbanism across this dynamic ground. ∆

Note

1. The term 'super-surface' refers to the array of hydrological infrastructures that support this highly calibrated landscape. At first glance this region might appear wholly bucolic and operating in another time period as farmers tiptoe through rice paddies amid ox-driven wagons. However, this region has an infrastructural excess, perhaps greater than that of the densest blocks of Hong Kong, Tokyo or Manhattan.

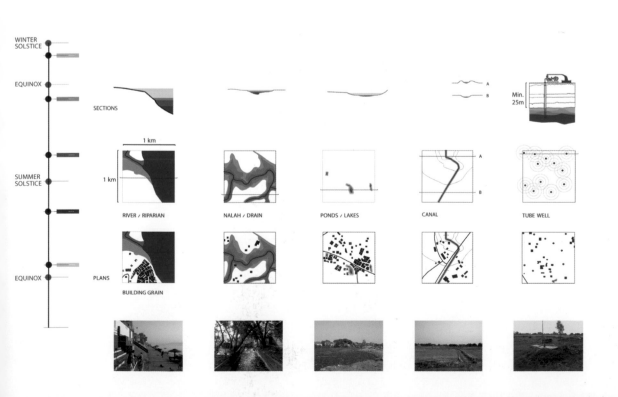

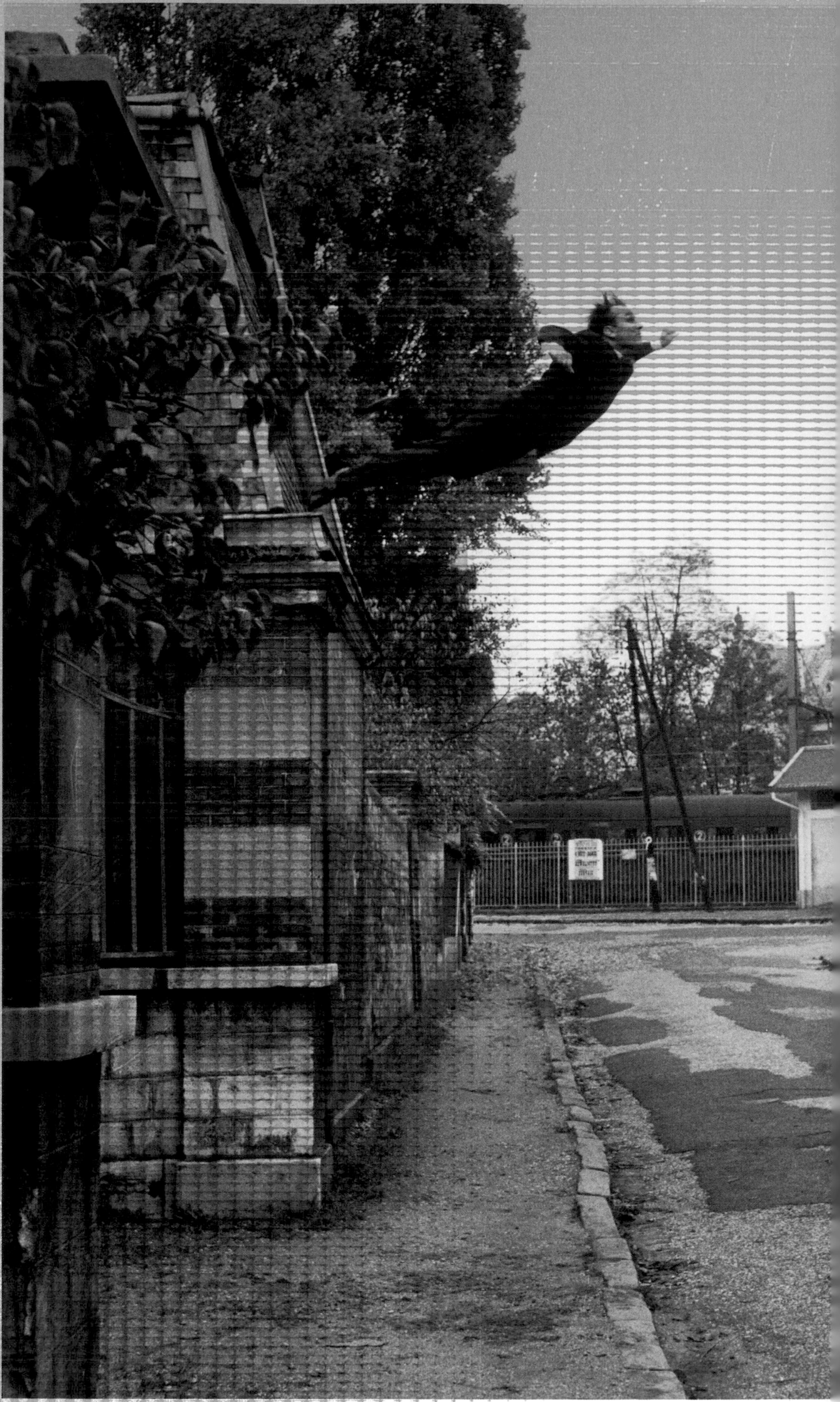

AFTER THE EVENT

SPECULATIVE PROJECTS IN THE AFTERMATH

Working on speculative architectural projects in the aftermath of traumatic events requires both fearlessness and sensitivity on the part of the designer. **Samantha Spurr** describes how architecture studios organised by the University of Technology, Sydney, held in Shenzhen, Berlin and Beirut, have brought students into direct contact with these issues and fragile sites.

Yves Klein, Leap into the Void, 1960
Klein's photo encapsulates the liberation and terror of the creative act. Subtitled 'Man in Space! The Painter of Space Throws himself into the Void', the collage shows Klein's own body suspended above the cobbled streetscape, on the cusp of either falling or flying.

Amanda Clarke, Ubiquitous City, Global Field Studio:
Shenzhen (tutors: Adrian Lahoud and Charles Rice),
University of Technology, Sydney, 2008
The Ubiquitous City series is a narrative projection of Buji
village, Shenzhen, after the introduction of the new rail
system. It explores the collapse of 'separate' systems –
logistical infrastructure, transport infrastructure, public
space, private space, residential and commercial – into one
heterogeneous system that differentiates both vertically and
horizontally without discrimination. While these paintings are
quite fantastical, this method of recording the city suggests
that the urban fabric has aspects that can only be revealed or
highlighted via subtle fabrications and iterations.

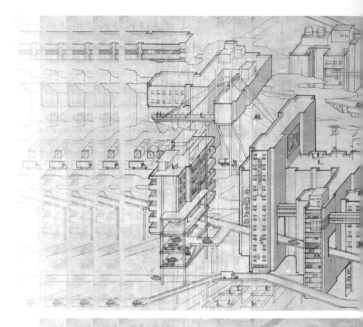

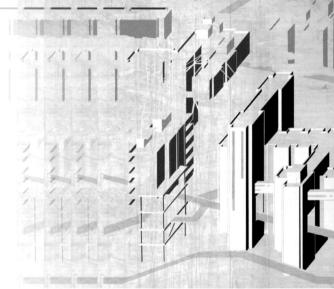

Post-traumatic urbanism defines a state of aftermath not
extremity. It is the uncanny stillness that comes after the
apocalypse, as captured in the bleak intensity of Cormac
McCarthy's book *The Road*.[1] Unlike the momentous
event, the post-traumatic aftermath elicits a focus on
survival, the desire for regeneration, the need for hope.
In the rubble of extreme social and material upheaval,
the resonating question is simply: 'What happens now?'

This question is the basis of speculative
architectural projects. From the Greek root of *theoria*,
meaning to look for something, 'to speculate' theorises
an existing scenario demanding critical and active
engagement. Speculative architectural projects search
for meanings using the tools and methods of the
architect. In turn, the production of such projects in the
fragile state of the post-traumatic demands two things:
fearlessness and sensitivity.

Encapsulated in the war cry of Henry V on the
bloody fields of Agincourt – 'Once more unto the breach,
dear friends, once more' – to be bold takes not only
courage, but determination. This is fearlessness. It is the
grainy photograph of French postwar artist Yves Klein's
outstretched body propelled above a Parisian street –
Leap into the Void (1960). It means putting oneself at
risk. To be sensitive is to be receptive and responsive
to the world we inhabit beyond moral categories.
The philosopher Elizabeth Grosz describes art as the
intensification of sensation, pinpointing a desire for life
to be more than simply about survival, but for it to be
resonant and vivid.[2]

The following projects are drawn from a series of
architecture studios at the University of Technology,
Sydney. Held in Shenzhen, Berlin and Beirut, the studios
brought students into direct and intimate collision with
these issues and the sites within which they occurred.

Outside of existing Chinese urban planning laws,
small farming and fishing villages have experienced
largely unconstrained development and growth since

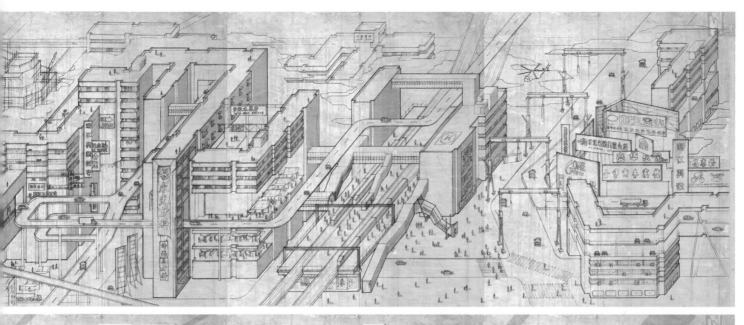

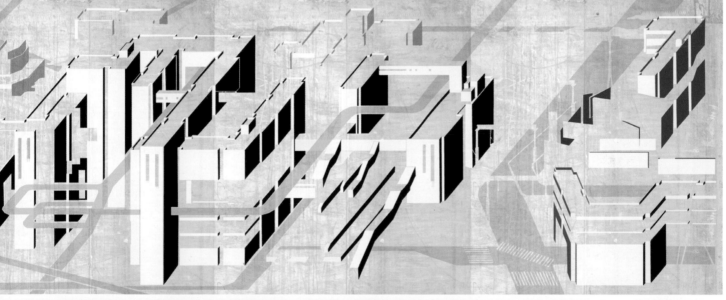

Jessica Paterson, Empty Lot Berlin, Social Transformations Studio (tutors: Adrian Lahoud and Samantha Spurr), University of Technology, Sydney, 2008
In this project sited on the border of Friedrichshain and Kreuzberg, Paterson has designed a residential typology of interlocked apartments in the creation of a new kind of Berlin-block. The permeable interface of the envelope is purposely eviscerated in the celebration of a singular form that offers no negotiation with its urban environment. Part architectural intervention and part commercial development proposal, the project explores the local focus on both gentrification and historic nostalgia.

The issue of memory as monument was taken up by Jessica Paterson in her Empty Lot Berlin project for the Social Transformations Studio (2008). The Berlin Wall has taken on a mythical status in the city's identity. At the same time the empty lots across central and east Berlin have become emblematic of the city's economic stasis.

Diana Hanna Hani, Beirut Ruins, Disciplinary
Transformations Studio (tutor: David Burns),
University of Technology, Sydney, 2009
below: The centuries-old ruins, located in
Bachoura in Beirut, are highly domesticated
spaces. Here they are transformed from a
private domestic space to an unencapsulated
voyeuristic space. The property remains private,
yet with the violent removal of their envelope
the ruins present themselves as a space with
a threshold that cannot be transgressed. The
space has been stripped bare of its privacy;
however its typological DNA means it can never
become public. The ruins remain in a state of
in-between, in the interstitial zone.

Diana Hanna Hani, Farouk Kork, Hugh
Irving, Samaneh Moafi, Grace Uy and Tobias
Robinson, Continuity, Social Transformations
Studio. University of Technology, Sydney, 2008
opposite: This project, in collaboration
with the staff and students of the American
University of Beirut, was generated through
the examination of the suburb of Bachoura
in Beirut, an inner-city area slated for radical
development and gentrification. The material
form of the site was systematically mapped
and documented, through which the social
and cultural issues enlivened by conversation
and engagement with local students were
embedded. This analysis exposed a complex
system of hierarchical boundaries demanding a
nuanced and thoughtful approach to integrating
continuity into an urban fabric.

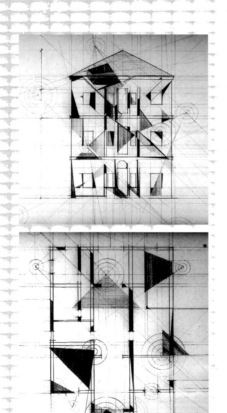

the beginning of Shenzhen's super-expansion in the early 1980s, resulting in the creation of dense urban enclaves. Accommodating itinerant workers from the countryside, the enclaves are slated for continuously up-scaled development; tenements devour family dwellings, in turn to be consumed by super-blocks. As part of the Global Field Studio: Shenzhen (March 2008), students spent two weeks investigating this distinctly new urban condition.

Appropriating the format of the Chinese scroll painting, Amanda Clarke's project Ubiquitous City presented a drab and endless urban cycle that subsumes each new community as it gains social purchase. In the demise of traditional social and spatial activities, the enclaves exude a strange reality; they are environments dedicated to development. Shenzhen's cycle of demolition and construction enacts a unique psychological state where the erasure of both past and future keeps the patient in a temporal vacuum, continuously repeating the traumatic moment. Clarke's triptych eloquently and meticulously reproduces the spatial symptoms of the enclaves, trapping the gaze in claustrophobic circulation.

Memory weighs heavily upon the post-traumatic city. In cities like Berlin and Beirut the past is tangible in the streetscape. The pedestrian walks through these memories, counting bullet holes and reciting texts nailed by doorways or inscribed in floors. The aesthetic seduction of these ruined states easily fuels a romanticised vision of the past, relegating thinking to the object and not the observer. Challenging the trope of the memorial as a container for memory, Diana Hanna Hani's project Beirut Ruins for the Disciplinary Transformations Studio (2009) exposes the voyeuristic consumption of the ruins. Engaging an intense sensitivity to the Beirut urban locale, her speculation on the role of memory in a city desirous of rapid development takes the mode of a finely tuned

architectural drawing. The drawings frame the ruined buildings, memorialising them through the image and in the process dislocating that memory from the material object. Refusing the role of the monument, Hani turns to the city itself for an authentic past. These images highlight the seductive nature of the ruptured facades, while the corresponding plans present the programmatic realities of these memorials – that they were once homes, personal and private spaces violently exposed by warfare and then again by geometries of vision.

The issue of memory as monument was taken up by Jessica Paterson in her Empty Lot Berlin project for the Social Transformations Studio (2008). The Berlin Wall has taken on a mythical status in the city's identity. At the same time the empty lots across central and east Berlin have become emblematic of the city's economic stasis. The paradox of the wall and the void are the premise of Paterson's project: the building constructed from the dissected limb of a neighbouring apartment block, the wall peeled diagonally away and cutting aggressively across the new site. The amplification of wall/apartment block into gargantuan proportions exemplifies the city's traumatic obsession, now more worthy of its Freudian objectification. In a blackly comic twist, the metaphor of the wall is reused as part of the suburb's bourgeoning gentrification.

The speculative project as urban design is commonly situated in either conventional practice or utopian fantasy. The student projects here were looking for an alternative process that engaged a critically optimistic premise from a contemporary real-world perspective. In direct response to Berlin's excessive monumentalisation of the past, or Beirut and Shenzhen's enforced amnesia in the face of rapid development, the students grappled with the possibilities of a specifically architectural engagement with memory. The projects sited in Beirut for the Social Transformations Studio questioned the relationship between spatial diversity

and social diversity. Analysis began with the typology of the traditional walk-up apartment, allowing for a careful analysis of culturally formed spatial intimacies – specifically familial arrangements and the gendered relationship of public and private environments.

The Beirut student project in Bachoura can be read as designing for a 'loose fit' – planning imbued with a suppleness to enable and make room for alternative spatial inhabitations and programmatic variations. Cities like Berlin and Beirut remain traumatised by the divisive effects of an urban-scale military demarcation that constituted, with such devastating personal consequences, a right and wrong side to be on. In Beirut, still so heavily bounded, delineated and dissected, the issue of continuity is understood as integral. In the aptly named Continuity project for the Social Transformations Studio, the gradient becomes a design tactic in the creation of transition across spaces. Mobility and access become the strategy for stitching back together the severed cultural and social fabric of the city.

Speculative design is not an endpoint; it questions rather than solves. An initial definition of post-traumatic urbanism might be the rapid and temporary response to a crisis scenario. However, the projects described here have sought to uncover longer-term issues, pursuing historical narratives, social memory and cultural interactions. In doing so they propose urban possibilities untethered to the immediate damaged reality, a willingness to explore different approaches and an awareness and concern for the unique and individual situations within these urban contexts. ᗪ

Notes
1. Cormac McCarthy, *The Road*, Vintage Books (New York), 2006.
2. Elizabeth Grosz, *Chaos, Territory, Art*, Columbia University Press (please provide city of publication), 2008.

Eyal Weizman
Paulo Tavares
Susan Schuppli
Situ Studio

Clyde Snow, the American forensic anthropologist and the flamboyant pioneer of the 'osteo-biography', here presents forensic evidence in the 1985 trial of members of the Argentine junta.

FORENSIC ARCHITECTURE

The urban destruction captured by black and white photos of London after the Blitz or bomb-damaged Berlin are emblematic of the desolation brought by modern warfare. **Eyal Weizman, Paulo Tavares, Susan Schuppli and Situ Studio** describe, though, how the built environment now represents more than a means of violation in conflict, as it has become an important source of evidence bearing witness to the event when international justice is sought.

Issues relating to the built environment are entering the courts and media forums of international justice with increasing frequency. This is because the built environment is both the means of violation and a source of evidence that can bear witness to the events that traversed it. Legal claims that are brought to international courts and tribunals or circulated within the mass media often include images of destroyed buildings or menacing structures. Too often, these structures or ruins are considered self-evident illustrations of atrocity. The field of forensic architecture must now emerge to attempt to transform the built environment from an illustration of alleged violations to a source of knowledge about historical events – or rather, as a complex methodology aimed at narrating histories from the things that it saturates.

Etymologically, 'forensics' is derived from a Latin term meaning 'before the forum' and refers to the practice and skill of making propositions through objects before professional and political gatherings or courts of law. Forensics thus belongs to the art of rhetoric; only here, it is the mediated speech of the object/thing, rather than people, that is addressed to the forums. In the contemporary period, the adjective 'forensic' refers to the legal application of scientific techniques. While emphasising the virtues of an objective, distant and disinterested approach, contemporary forensics also attempts to actualise historical relations as material ones.

Forensic architecture designates two interrelated sets of spatial relations: namely, the relation between an event and the spaces in which it is registered, and the relation between the evidence presented and the forum (such as the court or the media) that is sometimes called up and assembled by the evidence itself. Forensics is thus concerned both with the materialisation of the event and also with the performance of the object within a forum.

The contemporary forums to which forensic architecture addresses itself are also to be found beyond the actual spaces of the court; they are diffuse and interconnected, created through and by the media, and operate across a multiplicity of international institutions. The stakes of forensic analysis thus exceed the space of the law. International tribunals are not only places where evidence is presented and decisions are rendered, but they are also, following Laura Kurgan, broadcast studios, databases and historical archives.[1] The presentation of spatial evidence – as digital models, maps or simulations – should be conceptualised as introducing a new language into the legal process alongside older, more established forms of evidence, shifting spatial and knowledge relations.

The forensic sciences began to obtain their distinction within the framework of international law after the end of the Cold War, when international humanitarian law (IHL) became one of the primary domains for extensive research on conflict. Forensic

Slobodan Milošević's cross-examination of András Riedlmayer's expert testimony at the International Criminal Tribunal for the former Yugoslavia, The Hague, April 2002
Though it is not a rare thing to see an architectural professional meet a brutal political leader, here in an international tribunal this meeting designates a different relationship between politics and architecture. The exchange is indicative of the issues relating to reading rubble.

Slobodan Milošević: Do you know that the Hadum Mosque in Djakovica, which was not directly targeted by NATO … [was destroyed] when it targeted [other] places in Djakovica?

András Riedlmayer: … we found no signs that it had been subjected to explosive damage. … I am not a military expert, but I would suggest that somebody was using something other than an aerial missile to decapitate the minaret.

…

Milošević: As we quite obviously don't agree on that and you yourself said you are not a ballistic expert, do you really not consider that it would be a good idea for some experts to take a look at it and to entertain whether what I am claiming is the truth or whether your findings are the right ones?

archaeology and forensic anthropology are both relatively new disciplines that became prominent during the 1990s war crimes investigations in Yugoslavia and Argentina. This shift of emphasis in human rights and war crimes investigation meant that forensic science also began to gradually invade some of the legal (and cultural) territory previously reserved for testimony (mainly by victims).

Thomas Keenan mentioned the way in which some of the great gravediggers of the 1990s, such as Clyde Snow (who pioneered the forensic presentation of mass graves and also investigated the remains of people from Josef Mengele to Tutankhamun) and others were rather flamboyant in their presentation of the logic of what they were doing: Snow refers to his work as 'osteo-biography' saying, 'there is a brief but very useful and informative biography of an individual contained within the skeleton, if you know how to read it', or 'bones make great witnesses; they speak softly but they never forget and they never lie'.[2] But do they never lie?

The culture of human rights relies to a great extent upon the posture of the witness, and its contribution is unique in that it opens up the historical record to include previously excluded voices. If the forums of international law are now also opening up to the 'speech of things', this shift in epistemological emphasis would also designate a cultural and ethical transformation. New ways of using the forensic sciences have already begun to blur a previously held distinction: that between

Only the Criminal Can Solve the Crime: Marc Garlasco, former Human Rights Watch (HRW) 'expert on battle damage assessment', delivers a public forensic analysis of the bombing of Gaza, 2009
Between the end of the attack on Gaza and the summer of 2009, Marc Garlasco authored a series of reports demonstrating possible violation of international law by the Israeli military. His findings are quoted 36 times in the Goldstone report. Before joining HRW, Garlasco worked for seven years as an intelligence analyst in the US Defense Intelligence Agency at the Pentagon. He undertook target selection and planning for aerial bombing in the 1998 attack on Iraq, and the 1999 NATO attack on Serbia. Paradoxically or not, it was his military past that gained him the visibility and credibility he enjoyed as a human rights analyst, and also the methods of reading the rubble. In his reports, Garlasco attempts to read a certain system and order in the chaos of destruction: 'I needed to paste together the battle story.'

Head of the UN Fact Finding Mission Justice Richard Goldstone holds a press conference, Gaza, June 2009
The most intense example of the emergent relationship between architecture and law through forensics is the legal and diplomatic furore around the publication of Richard Goldstone's 'Report of the United Nations Fact Finding Mission on the Gaza Conflict', which alleges that the Israeli army and Hamas have committed war crimes. In this image Goldstone stands in front of the destruction of a tall building. Beside him are members of the government in Gaza, and the microphones of places worldwide are in front of him. He seems to speak on behalf of the rubble. Here the ruin seems to assemble a 'formless' forum around which the object is made to speak.

evidence – where the law speaks of objects – and witnesses, in which case it speaks of human beings. If material evidence, then, is conceptually understood, technically unveiled and legally acknowledged as also being capable of some 'speech', then witnesses of the non-human variety could be interrogated and cross-examined – and even 'lie' in the sense of offering the potential for multiple, contradictory scenarios. We therefore need another tentative extension to the definition of forensics, one that can be understood as the process by which material evidence turns into what could be called 'material witness', entailing that objects have some agency and that experts act as its translators. The category of 'material witness' must thus be formally reintroduced as occupying the ground between an object and a subject.

In forensic architecture, the object/thing or structure should not be seen in isolation, but as a part of a complex assemblage, networked into ever shifting sets of relations – people, spaces and other things, humans and non-human, that are holding together social and political relations. Things are never really static. If things are under constant transformation and interlinking, then politics should be understood as matter in movement. Forensic architecture thus conceives of spaces/events as material and temporal hybrids distributed throughout the entire architectural field, and the built environments as being beyond merely the

Images from the archive compiled by the Palestinian Ministry of Public Works and Housing in the Gaza Strip. Both photos are of buildings destroyed on 15 January 2009 in the As-Salam neighbourhood of North Jabaliya. The date of inspection was some three to four months after the buildings were bulldozed and bombed by Israeli forces Israel's 21-day assault on the Gaza Strip in winter 2008/09 killed almost 1,400 people and destroyed or damaged about 16,000 buildings – 15 per cent of all the buildings in Gaza. Most of the people killed died inside buildings, many in their own homes. In the wake of the attack, the Ministry of Public Works and Housing for Gaza began producing an archive that catalogued the destroyed structures. In the archive, each damaged or destroyed home, house, ministry, school or clinic was designated with a catalogue number. The numbers were spray-painted onto the ruins themselves, and catalogued in a vast 'book of destruction' with the same number. The logic of the archive is that of a systematic property damage survey – a practical way to account for the necessary work of rebuilding, and its cost. In its dry, disembodied and bureaucratic logic, its surveyors' photographs, diagrams and captions, it might be the necessary, perhaps even the only possible response to the magnitude of the scale of Gaza destruction. Moreover, because buildings were here used as weapons, the destroyed structures become the material witnesses to the logic of the attack and the chaos of its violence.

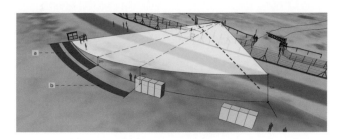

sites of, or the backdrops to, violation, rather as protagonists in the unfolding of incidents.

It is in this sense and others that forensic architecture is elusive and contingent. Rather than operating as the mechanical materialisation of time, or as the conclusive, objective apparatus of truth claims, it is inclined towards complex, sometimes unstable and even contradictory accounts of events as it navigates the murky ground of a 'fuzzy' forensics of probabilities, possibilities and interpretations.

It is this feature that allows forensic architecture to produce 'an archaeology of the present' unpacking present histories in order to critically engage with the dynamics of political events as they are unfolding.

It has also a lesson for both fields of architecture and law. The 'architecture' in 'forensic architecture' does not designate the product of building design, but an expanded field of spatial investigation and enquiry. The adjective 'forensic' can be understood as the very condition that enables architecture to become a diagnostic technique, whereby immaterial forces are made manifest themselves. ⌂

Notes

1. Laura Kurgan, 'Residues: ICTY Courtroom No 1 and the Architecture of Justice, in Len Guenther and Cornelius Heesters (eds), *Alphabet City 7*: Social Insecurity, 2000, pp 112–30.
2. Thomas Keenan and Eyal Weizman in conversation. ArteEast/Parsons School for Design, New York, 13 February 2010.

Situ Studio, 3-D virtual model reconstruction of the scene at the moment of the shooting, 2010
Image of the report initiated at the request of Attorney Michael Sfard and the Israeli Human Rights organisation B'Tselem to reconstruct the events of the 17 April 2009 protest at Bil'in in which a protestor, Bassem Ibrahim Abu Rahma, was struck and killed by a tear gas grenade. The height of the yellow virtual plane above the ground on the Israeli Defense Force side of the fence limits the possible locations that the shot could have been fired from. Up to 2 metres high is the zone from which a direct shot could have been fired. Up to 4 metres high, as defined by the intersection of the plane with fence 1, is the zone at which a deflection with the fence could have occurred. At the lowest limit of this zone at which a deflection could have been occurred, a section is taken to determine the angle of firing of the projectile. After analysing available video footage of the event and conducting a series of calculations at various launch angles it appears highly improbable that the lethal round was discharged at 60 degrees or above (the minimum angle specified in the Israel Defense Force's own Open Fire Regulations for indirect fire).

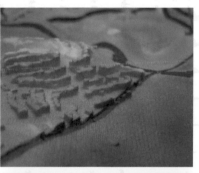

Model showing proposed boundaries of the path of the Wall in the West Bank and depiction by Christine Cornell of the Israeli High Court of Justice referring to a model
The series of interrelated legal challenges that dealt with the wall in the Israeli High Court of Justice were not criminal trials in the sense of seeking to establish individual guilt and punishments, but rather a set of legal processes to configure and regulate the properties of an apparatus. These were thus not trials of people but those of 'things', as it was the 'behaviour' of the Wall that was debated using models and testimonies. In these legal processes expert witnesses testifying for the security, humanitarian, nutritional and agricultural implication of the project, state and military agents, human rights lawyers and even the Palestinians directly affected by it, engaged in a process of fine-tuning the details and path of the Wall and its associated regime. This legal/design process was set to establish a proportional relation between seemingly conflicting demands: calculating the path of the Wall in the West Bank so that it mediates between what state agents sought to define as its vital security needs and what the humanitarian lawyers were willing to concede were the excessive negative implications on the livelihood of people living along it. It is through the structure of the legal argument that the model has become implicated in the design process, and it is through the model that the law got mobilised in material action. The legal discourse meant that a certain 'forensic engineering' came into play – the Wall was designed in court.

Tarsha Finney

THE INFRASTRUCTURE OF STABILITY

A US Army Chinook helicopter sits on the tarmac at the Bagram airbase, Afghanistan, 20 September 2006. US and NATO troops had been involved in a series of offensives since the spring of that year to quell a spreading Taliban insurgency and spark reconstruction efforts.

Afghanistan's key strategical position, lying between Asia and the Middle East, has made it prey to foreign invasion throughout its history. **Tarsha Finney** explains how an existing military infrastructure of airports, roads, accommodation and unskilled concentrations of labour have given the US and its allies an important leg-up in the current conflict, providing what could be perceived to be an underlying structure of stability.

Since 2001, argument in the US over strategy in Afghanistan has lurched between the contradictory doctrines of surge and exit. Like a high-stakes game of poker, to play is to raise or fold. To make a minimum bet and stay in the game is to not really play at all. In Afghanistan, those real men of decisive action want a radical increase in troop numbers and a swift Taliban defeat; or they want an immediate exit and some relief from troop casualties and the sheer financial burden of involvement.

Despite this, however, the idea of a minimum bet to stay in the game has been gaining ground. This radical strategy, what is being called a 'long war', involves a much reduced but longer-term engagement of between five and 10 years. Here, Afghanistan is understood as a strategic chapter within a wider conflict which also involves Iraq, Pakistan and even insurgency front lines within European communities where Dr David Kilcullen, counterinsurgency expert, argues that human rights laws create legislative 'safe havens' for urban insurgency undergrounds. Kilcullen, credited with the idea of the long war, sits in direct opposition to Donald Rumsfeld's tactics of 'shock and awe' implemented in the early days of the 2001 US campaign in Afghanistan, where the emphasis was on technology, long-range fire power and spectacular displays of force.

Kilcullen earned a doctorate in political anthropology from the University of New South Wales. His thesis studied the effects of insurgency warfare on non-state political systems in traditional societies, particularly the 1950s and 1960s Darul Islam conflict between the Indonesian government and a Muslim insurgency movement. For him, counterinsurgency can be defined as a zone between an excess of combat power which cannot or should not be used on a population, and the failure of all other means to secure the 'hearts, minds and acquiescence' of that population.[1] The key to that zone, he believes, is anthropology and sociology. Among his contributions to the discussion is the idea that 'people don't get pushed into rebellion by their ideology', no matter what Italian filmmaker

Gillo Pontecorvo's mid-1960s classic *The Battle of Algiers* suggests. Rather, Kilcullen argues, 'they get pulled in'[2] by a cocktail mix of social networks and disaffection. It is within the context of these new ways of thinking that we can begin to see quite differently the infrastructural inheritance of a theatre of war like Afghanistan. It is an inheritance that tends much more towards stability than disruption.

Afghanistan is worn with occupation. Long periods at war are part of its history. Whether overtly military or simply territorial in ambition, to list the tidal flow of incoming interests requires fortitude. To acknowledge just a few: the Anglo-Afghan wars of 1839 and 1878, the 1979–89 Soviet occupation, or those interventions and foreign occupations that arrived via mid-20th-century international development aid infrastructure: the international airport at Kandahar built by US civilian finance in the 1960s, for example. This was developed as a refuelling port for long-range flights between the Middle East and Asia, and then used by both the Soviets and the US in the later decades of the 20th century as a key military installation. As a consequence, in every direction in Afghanistan a constellation of military infrastructure and broken hardware overlays the country, detritus of this history of occupation. And with a surprising irony, it is this infrastructure that has given each incoming force, including the US and its 40-strong International Security Assistance Force (ISAF) allies, a leg-up in the country: airports, roads, abandoned military aircraft and accommodation, and ready-positioned unskilled labour concentrations for use by international civilian contractors. Mainstream media reports about this country would have us understand it as Stone Aged, with its mud-brick houses, unpaved roads and absence of a blanket grid of electricity – evidence of its apparent lack of capacity to engage in modern warfare. Yet in urban infrastructure terms, it is far from that.

Take, for example, the Bagram airbase, or Bagram Airfield as it is formally known by the US military, 64 kilometres (40 miles) northwest of Kabul. It was built by the Soviets as early as the 1960s and was used throughout their occupation from 1979 to 1989. Contested by the Taliban and Afghan Northern Alliance throughout the civil war era, the air-traffic control tower reportedly served as a media-briefing site by a Northern Alliance general. Bagram airbase is now one of the key military installations for the US, housing civilian and military medical facilities as well as the notorious Bagram prison with its 750 mostly Taliban inmates, of whom 30 were brought to Afghanistan from outside the country. Bagram airbase sits along side Guantanamo Bay and Abu Ghraib prison on an international itinerary of questionable US correctional facilities.

Under US administration, the airbase has been expanding since 2001, leveraging off of its Soviet-built core. It is now a 2,100-hectare (5,189-acre) compound that includes shops,

Destroyed Soviet fighter planes
lie near stacks of supplies for
the US military at the Bagram
airbase, 5 April 2002.

above: Soldiers from the opposition Northern Alliance stand beside one of several old MIG jet fighters on the Bagram airbase, 4 October 2001.

right: Afghan men look at photographs in an English-language magazine on 22 March 2002 while sifting through the area that is being used as the waste dump on the Bagram airbase. The garbage, which is produced by the coalition forces at the base, is a combination of discarded MREs, paper, bottles, food products and other waste. Local Afghans await each truckload of garbage daily in anticipation of sifting through for any salvageable goods.

What is fascinating about Afghanistan is that each of these infrastructural capacities – hardware, labour, airports, marketplaces – thicken and densify in surprising ways and assist Afghanistan's tacit support for each new game-player on its territory.

restaurants, 3 kilometres (1.86 miles) of aircraft runway, offices and barracks, and it is a key component of the 16,093-kilometre (10,000-mile) aerobridge that runs between the US mainland and Afghanistan, from the concrete runways of Charleston Air Force Base, South Carolina, to the airfields of Bagram, Kandahar and Shin. Since late 2009 this aerobridge has operated as part of the latest surge. More than 30,000 troops and up to 60,000 tonnes of cargo and supplies have moved via the only secure route between these two places – direct air. Hardware fetishists might like to note that up to 20 times a day, C-5A Galaxies and C-17 aircraft, each able to carry the equivalent contents of four 18-wheeled trucks, fly direct between the US mainland and these Soviet-built airbases of southern and central Afghanistan.

What is fascinating about Afghanistan is that each of these infrastructural capacities – hardware, labour, airports, marketplaces – thicken and densify in surprising ways and assist Afghanistan's tacit support for each new game-player on its territory. These are unaligned skilled economies that develop around wars. They shift from side to side irrespective of outcome and eventual master. Take the aircraft used to resupply the growing US military presence in the country in the later months of 2001. These were commercial Russian-made IL76s and AN12s, manned by crew from the ex-Soviet Union working for civilian supply companies contracted to the US military. These aircraft and the individuals crewing them had gained direct and invaluable knowledge of Afghanistan via involvement in the preceding Soviet occupation of the late 1970s and 1980s, a conflict, which involved a CIA-backed Taliban, galvanised against the Russians. In 2001 these planes operated from the United Arab Emirates, the key transport hub for US and European airfreight. The IL76, with its internal crane and capacity to drop a 6-metre (20-foot) container directly on to a runway, thereby doing away with ground support, was ideal for the job in Afghanistan. As non-US flagged aircraft, to have one of these planes go down, unlike the loss of an American-registered aircraft, was not newsworthy to a voracious media focused on US losses for an anxious attention-deficit public back home.

At the main entry gate to the Bagram airfield, on the road that runs from Bagram to Kabul, sits the village of Bagram. In 2001 this village had a population of approximately 5,000 people; today it is significantly larger. Bagram village emerged during the time of the Soviet occupation to house the unskilled labour, merchants and their families who survive off and profit from the presence of the base. Currently living here are thousands of Afghani civilians who daily, like they did for the Soviets before, work as unskilled labour for the international civilian contractors tasked with servicing the airbase, supporting the US military as cleaners, janitors and

unskilled construction workers. Legend has it that when there are VIPs on the base, such as Dick Cheney in 2009, for obvious security reasons this minor army of support staff are kept off the base for the duration of the visit. Within hours things start to slow down: the toilets don't get cleaned, the mess halls don't get cleaned, the expansion plans which include multistorey concrete accommodation blocks for the increased troop numbers expected as part of the current surge don't get built.

Servicing both the airbase and the village of Bagram is a market. Just as the unaligned skilled economies of invasion logistics shift from side to side irrespective of master, so the edge condition of the base bleeds information with a porosity that challenges traditional notions of taking sides. In this market it is possible to buy almost anything that is available on the base: electrical goods, furniture, food, sporting equipment. How it gets there no one seems to know – or be prepared to tell. There are reports that at certain times it has even been possible to buy bags of USB sticks containing random information regarding life and the workings of the military at the base. It is unclear from the reports as to whether these USB sticks were stolen with information already in place, or if they were taken in and used as repositories for information downloaded. Either way, the social security details of all four of the highest-ranking officers on the base have to be worth something to someone.

Regardless of the strategy eventually followed in Afghanistan – surge, withdrawal or long play – this conflict and the knowledge fields of anthropology and sociology that are being newly deployed in its interest afford us the opportunity to see infrastructural capacities differently, be they airports, roads, housing or labour. Kilcullen's investigations show us that the ideological categories and distinctions that we typically use to organise our understandings of urban infrastructure and its context of conflict don't hold here. There is instead a different kind of porosity and elasticity to what is in effect an infrastructure of long-term stability. ◬

Notes
1. David Kilcullen, 'Twenty-Eight Articles: Fundamentals of Company-level Counterinsurgency', *Military Review*, Vol 86, Issue 3, May 2006, pp 103–06.
2. See George Packer, 'Knowing the Enemy: Can Social Scientists redefine the "war on terror"?', *The New Yorker*, 18 December 2006. See www.newyorker.com/archive/2006/12/18/061218fa_fact2, accessed 7 May 2010.

Mark Fisher

POST-APOCALYPSE NOW

In cinema, the post-apocalypse has become a recurring theme offering endless opportunities to envisage and keep on reimagining the end of the world as we know it. Here **Mark Fisher** explores the post-apocalyptic in Children of Men (2006), The Road (2006) and Terminator Salvation (2009), and asks whether these seminal films point towards a tendency to imagine the end of existence over the end of capitalism.

McG, *Terminator Salvation*, 2009
The desolated CGI landscape of McG's
Terminator Salvation fits with the burned-
out ideological terrain of the world after the
financial crisis.

The question that hangs over Alfonso Cuarón's 2006 film *Children of Men* is: has the catastrophe already happened? Or is it about to happen? Or does the particular form of catastrophe in question resist any kind of periodisation? The crisis is as unexplained as it is total: there has been a failure of fertility, so that no children have been born for a generation. The catastrophe, therefore, is not a punctual event so much as an ongoing decline: the world ending as a long drawn-out whimper. The premise of any number of previous post-apocalyptic fictions is undercut, because in *Children of Men*, the moment of apocalypse and of post-apocalypse are coterminous. There is no question of surviving the catastrophe and reconstructing society afterwards. With no coming generations, there is, evidently, no one to reconstruct society for, nor anyone to continue the work of reconstruction. The catastrophe, in fact, *consists* in this failure of the future, this absence of continuity.

One of the most powerful scenes takes place inside Battersea Power Station, which now functions as a 'Ministry of Art', in which the elite preserve and enjoy cultural treasures (Picasso's *Guernica*, Velázquez's *Las Meninas*, Pink Floyd's inflatable pig). The lead character, Theo (Clive Owen) asks his cousin, Nigel, one of the ministry's curators, what the point of it all is if, in a hundred years, there won't be anyone left to see any of it. Nigel's answer exemplifies a kind of suave nihilism: 'You know what it is, Theo. I just don't think about it.' Without any possible connection to the future, cultural objects become museum pieces, a set of decontextualised ornaments (which can, of course, be recombined at will). The Ministry of Art, we can't help but feel, is an image of Postmodern culture itself – a culture that, as the Marxist cultural critic Fredric Jameson persuasively argued, is characterised by a tendency towards retrospection and pastiche. Is this, then, our post-apocalypse, the apocalypse proper to a Postmodernism which Jameson called 'the cultural logic of late capitalism'?[1] Will there really never be anything new again? Or can we only expect more of the same, forever?

John Hillcoat's 2009 adaptation of Cormac McCarthy's novel *The Road* (2006) does not even hold open the picturesque pleasures of dereliction that *Children of Men* offers. Here, just as in *Children of Men*, the catastrophe is never explained. But it works quite differently. Whereas the malaise in *Children of Men* affects only humans, leaving nature (beautifully shot by cinematographer Emmanuel Lubezki) unmolested, in *The Road* it is nature itself that dies. The ultimate effect is the same, however: there is no future.

Culture has literally been stripped away – there are few signs (in any sense) of the commodity system that once reigned over the planet. The houses that remain are gutted; the images on billboards have, for the most part, long since been effaced as humanity descends from the cybernetic empire of signs back into animality. When the two lead characters, the unnamed 'man' and his son, discover a can of Coke, it is a holy relic from a lost regime of commodity fetishism. The world may be ending, and capitalism may be over, but *The Road* does nothing to undermine the truth of Jameson's famous claim that 'it is easier to imagine the end of the world than the end of capitalism'.[2]

The Road's end of the world has terminated capitalism, but it does not clear a space for any sort of alternative to it. Despite the seemingly redemptive flavour of the film's final scene (in which the orphaned boy is taken on by another family), the theme of post-apocalyptic reconstruction is as redundant in *The Road* as it is in *Children of Men*. To reproduce means only to extend the process of extinction, and, in any case there is nothing to reconstruct with, since both nature and the products of dead labour are close to being totally used up. In *The Road*, as in *Children of Men*, the old Leninist question 'What is to be done' has no possible purchase.

The theorist Jean-Pierre Dupuy has argued that the only way for us to avert an ecological catastrophe is for us to put ourselves into the position where it has already happened and ask: What we would have done to have avoided it?[3] As the Marxist philosopher Slavoj Žižek has suggested, the problem with accepting eco-catastrophe as a realistic possibility is that our everyday experience of the life-world contradicts what science tells us: 'Common sense finds it difficult to really accept that the flow of everyday reality can be perturbed … It is enough to see the natural world to which my mind is connected: green grass and trees, the sighing of the breeze, the rising of the sun … can one really imagine that this will be disturbed?'[4] The potentially political function of *The Road* then, arises from its removal of green grass and trees, prompting us to confront what everyday life would be like when the life-world is dead.

McG's *Terminator Salvation* (2009) offers another version of Dupuy's gambit. We are finally plunged into the midst of the future-world conflict between Skynet and the human population that we have only seen glimpses of in the previous films in the series. Here, CGI finally codes for cybergothic. If *Children of Men* captures the pre-2008 feeling of neoliberalism's inertial vaingloriousness (there is no future but this, for ever), then *Terminator Salvation*'s burned-out world, its scorched-earth terrain patched together out of a black metal artificial nightmare, is strikingly in tune with the derelicted ideological terrain after the financial crisis. Now that '[t]he assumptions that ruled policy and politics over three decades suddenly look as outdated as revolutionary socialism',[5] neoliberalism is in a 'dilapidated state' and its 'former pretensions to intellectual superiority and realism will no longer be sufferable'.[6] If, as *Terminator Salvation*'s pulp existentialist slogan has it, 'there is no fate but what we make', that's not because everything is possible again, but because everything – very much including what is left of the status quo – is suddenly impossible. The 'only possible way' has collapsed, and all that's left is an ideological landscape strewn with relics and junk. ∆

Notes
1. Fredric Jameson, *Postmodernism, or the Cultural Logic of Late Capitalism*, Verso (London and New York), 1992. For the arguments on retrospection and pastiche, see especially 'The Cultural Logic of Late Capitalism', pp 1–54.
2. Fredric Jameson, 'Future City', *New Left Review 21*, May/June 2003, pp 65–79. Jameson actually attributes the observation to an unnamed source: 'Someone once said that it is easier to imagine the end of the world than to imagine the end of capitalism.'
3. Jean-Pierre Dupuy, *Petite métaphysique des tsunami*, Seuil (Paris), 2005.
4. Slavoj Žižek, *In Defense of Lost Causes*, Verso (London and New York), 2009, p 465.
5. Martin Wolf, 'Seeds of its Own Destruction', *Financial Times*, 8 March 2009; see www.ft.com/cms/s/0/c6c5bd36-0c0c-11de-b87d-0000779fd2ac.html.
6. Gopal Balakrishnan, 'Speculations on the Stationary State', *New Left Review 59*, September/October 2009, pp 5–26.

Tony Chakar

THE EIGHTH DAY

GOD CREATED THE WORLD IN SEVEN DAYS. THIS IS THE EIGHTH DAY

Beirut-born architect and writer **Tony Chakar** describes how the July 2006 Israeli attacks on Beirut prompted memories of the Lebanese War and provided the essential catalyst for producing his work The Eighth Day. Careful not to stipulate prescribed meanings, Chakar delivers the series of images as a lecture that provide luminosity in 'the space of catastrophe' where 'language is undone'.

Tony Chakar, 'Breathe' photo-essay from The Eighth Day, Lebanon, 2009
opposite

Few will be able to guess how sad one had to be in order to resuscitate Carthage.
— Gustave Flaubert[1]

... even the dead will not be safe from the enemy if he wins. And this enemy has not ceased to be victorious.
— Walter Benjamin[2]

In July 2006, during the Israeli attacks on Lebanon, those of us who were fortunate enough to live in relatively safe areas had a distinct and eerie feeling of the war coming back. By 'war' is meant the Lebanese Wars of 1975 to 1990, during which at least 200,000 people were killed. We knew that war was there when Beirut became again an upside-down city, a city of unrelated points and infinite calculations, a city of borrowed and inverted dreams. War was there in the return of wartime reflexes; simple ones, like economising on water (although there was not really a water shortage), or avoiding walking in uncovered, 'unprotected' areas, or stocking up on canned food and so on. But war was also there in different ways as well, more imperceptible and insidious: our present was flooded with wartime images, and every object, every detail, acquired an allegorical meaning that was extraneous to its everyday one. Cars became again a source of potential danger, buckets were again seen as potential bathing tools, and we were again inventing rituals to appease

the telephone gods in order to get a line. All our actions were logical, all our actions were irrational, like in a dream.

All our space was inside, an inside that had no outside, like a dream. And like in a dream, we lived in a time warp for a couple of months, where the past invaded the present and where the present had no future.

This is when work began on The Eighth Day – a title that the work will acquire at a much later stage. The idea of the work was simple: what should be done with these images from the past bursting into the present? It was first necessary to collect them – not the images per se because they did not have any physical existence, but objects that generated them, objects that were attached to them. The process itself opened the door to more and more questions. What is the significance of these images and objects, and what is their meaning? Will the objects generate the same images if placed in a 'normal' space? Why are they linked to this particular past (the past of the Lebanese Wars) and not some other period? How will they cross the line from being personal objects into becoming public ones (and the worst kind of public objects – those associated with the dreaded realm of 'art', whatever that may be)?

From a simple beginning the project was demanding more and more complex answers. It was important not to fall into the trap of an audience's scopophilic desire to know more, to be informed more, to define exactly. In this

sense, The Eighth Day does not provide any quantifiable knowledge, any insight leading to an objective understanding of a war experience. It does not even pretend to talk about the war, or how people who were caught in it felt, or what they experienced. It does not present the audience with small everyday details and minute experiences in order to avoid a grand narrative. Instead it talks about something else, because talking about the thing itself will only make it banal and trivial – and in any case, what was experienced between 1975 and 1990, or its reappearance as evanescent images in 2006 and later in 2008, is too deep, too painful, too catastrophic to be verbalised or represented.

The Eighth Day operates like a constellation or, to use a more recent physics metaphor, it operates like a galaxy: every object collected, be it an image, a song, a newspaper clipping, a graffiti, a fragment from a movie or a contemporary art installation, a part of a text or a poem – they are all luminous points, stars in this galaxy, hovering around a centre, a black hole. The black hole cannot be seen or described in any way, but its existence is known because of the way its gravitational field affects the movement of the stars around it. And even though The Eighth Day takes the form of a lecture – or a lecture performance, or an artist talk, or a performance – the difficulty in describing this particular work is not without meaning. It operates more like a force field than a

This language cannot be the language of facts, numbers and statistics, like the one used by Hezbollah, for instance, in the party's assessment of the July 2006 attacks. This factual language is precisely the most incapable tool for seizing upon the evanescent images of the past due to their allegorical nature.

Tony Chakar,
'Breathe' photo-essay
from The Eighth Day,
Lebanon, 2009
above

Paul Klee, *Angelus
Novus*, 1920
opposite

lecture. Every evanescent image from the past is recognised, seized upon and held for a brief moment, stopping it from disappearing forever. Every image, be it an image-thought, an image-text, an image-wish, an image-promise, becomes a flickering luminous point, establishing relations with other images, and indicating that which cannot be said.

'That which cannot be said', not only because of the reasons stated above, and not because it is traumatic to the psyche of the individuals who experienced it; the war is not simply an individual experience, it is indeed a collective one. Not only does it destroy buildings and kill people, war destroys language itself, thus destroying one of the main elements that ensure the cohesiveness of this collective. In the space of catastrophe, language is undone, and words become more and more distant from what they are meant to designate. In 1985, three years after the 1982 Israeli invasion of Lebanon and amid the ongoing civil wars, Jocelyne Saab directed a movie entitled *A Suspended Life*. One of the scenes in the film is set against the backdrop of the utterly destroyed Beirut Sport City, the pride of 1950s International Style architecture. Two young girls are walking among the ruins, and one of them wants to talk about the man, a 30-something artist, she is madly in love with. But how will she find the language to talk about love in these ruins? She cannot, because that language has withdrawn. So after circling around the subject, she starts borrowing another

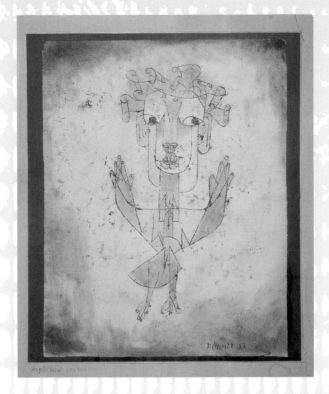

language: the language of love as it is spoken in popular Egyptian movies, with fragments and semi-sentences that have become extremely popular over the years: 'Say hello to the aubergines' or 'The honour of a girl is like a matchstick; it can only be lit once.'

Another example, much more poignant and straight to the point, would be Burhan Alawiya's 1981 film *Bayrut al-Liqaa* (*Beirut, The Meeting*, dialogues by Ahmad Baydoun), a story about two lovers, one in west Beirut and the other in the east, attempting to meet somewhere in the city, to no avail. In the end they decide to record audiotapes for each other. What is said in one of the tapes is worth quoting in full:

… what I have to do is much more difficult than before, because the dictionary has been wrecked; ask someone who would use a word three years ago what it means now … he has to come up with some other meaning. Certain words, Zeina, came to mean destruction and 60,000 people killed …

He then goes on to say:

who would have thought? And between you and me, I don't want to say that there are 60,000 bodies, but between you and me, and between any two people who are trying to meet in Beirut, there are a quarter of

a million cars, and 2,000 dumpsters, and a million words on the walls, and bullets and bodies and voices … when I talk to you, my words go through all of these people and these things, and I wonder what you understand.[3]

In the space of catastrophe, everything can mean anything else.

And he said to me: Prophesy to the breath, prophesy, son of man, and say to the breath, Thus says the Lord God: Come from the four winds, O breath, and breathe upon these slain, that they may live.[4]

After the war is over (whatever that means), what has been broken does not simply repair itself. We have on our hands a huge pile of linguistic debris, of hollowed-out words and broken phrases that have the bad habit of never really coinciding with their intended meanings, of falling to the ground before reaching their interlocutor. And it is no coincidence that a Lebanese rock group, in a song from 2008, used practically the same metaphor from a film made probably before they were born: 'Between you and me there are two million [people].'[5] But the past has a claim on us, and the destruction of language does not mean – cannot mean – that there is no possibility of talking about this past, of finding a language to speak the

space of catastrophe. This language cannot be the language of facts, numbers and statistics, like the one used by Hezbollah, for instance, in the party's assessment of the July 2006 attacks. This factual language is precisely the most incapable tool for seizing upon the evanescent images of the past due to their allegorical nature. And while the semi-scientific pretences of statistics aim to define, settle and appease the uncertainties of allegory and to give a seeming coherence to the linguistic rubble, other strategies are possible: the use of image-texts (the duality between image and text, of form and idea is a relatively new one), of poetry (in the Heideggerian sense of poetry as an instrument for measuring), of aphorisms (aphorisms being the perfect linguistic fragments, so to speak), to name but a few, could be a way to recognise the space of the past for what it really is: a space of catastrophe. ∆

Notes
1. Gustave Flaubert quoted in Walter Benjamin, 'On the Concept of History', in Hannah Arendt (ed), *Illuminations*, Schocken Books (New York), 1968, p 256.
2. Walter Benjamin, op cit, p 255.
3. Burhan Alawiya, *Beyrouth La Rencontre* (*Beirut, The Meeting*; Bayrut al-Liqaa), Belgium, Tunisia, Lebanon, 1981.
4. Ezekiel 37:9.
5. The group is called Mashrou' Leila (Leila's Project), and the metaphor is in reference to the two huge demonstrations of 8 and 14 March 2005, each claiming to gather more than a million demonstrators.

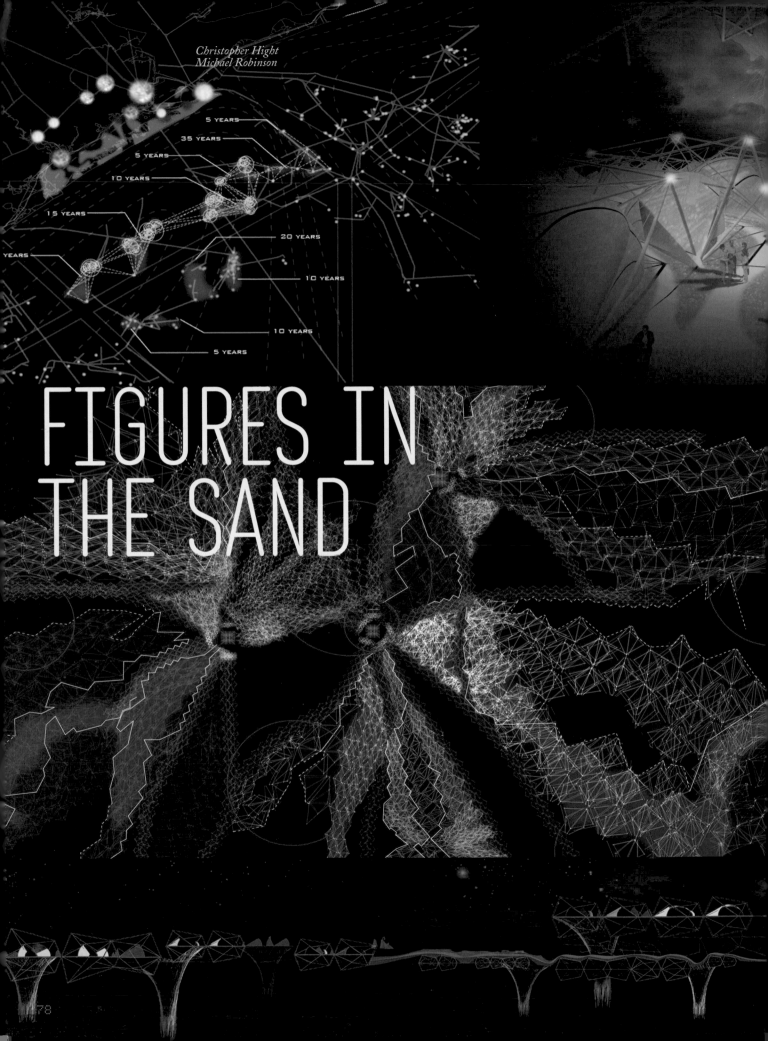

Christopher Hight
Michael Robinson

FIGURES IN
THE SAND

Coastal regions have become a magnet for recent development and globalisation, most conspicuously with the artificial islands off Dubai. This is a trend that has been offset by natural disasters, such as the tsunami and Hurricane Katrina. **Christopher Hight and Michael Robinson** describe how the Last Resort design studio at Rice School of Architecture has made its research focus Galveston Island, a nexus of natural, cultural and economic forces.

Just as agoraphobia is understood as resulting from the trauma of industrialisation and urbanisation in the late 19th- and early 20th-century metropolis, in the 21st century new phobias and subjects will arise along the periphery of the continents and out of the entangling of urbanisation with ecology. Over half of the US population lives near the coast;[1] globally, an estimated 2.75 billion people will live near the ocean's edge by 2025. Perhaps not unlike the mercantile cities of Venice and Lisbon, such places often have more in common with each other than the cities that lie on their territorial interior. This global coastal zone, or littoral, will increasingly manifest the political ecologies of the 21st century, combining issues of global capital, population growth, patterns of development, climate change and natural disasters.

Indeed, the inaugural decade of the millennium was characterised by two complementary sets of images. Global architectural culture met with neocolonial glee in the gleaming towers and artificial islands constructed along the coasts of the United Arab Emirates and the People's Republic of China: the iconic Palm and World resort communities in Dubai are artificial islands constructed in the shape of a logo for a lifestyle immersed in techno-nature as an ambient brand; Dongtan promised to be an instant eco-city on the sea. In these green urban confections, coastal development becomes not only isomorphic with, but also integral to, the advancement of global capital over the forms of political representation and economies of the 19th-century metropolis. On the other hand, the 24-hour media cycle has documented a seemingly unprecedented series of natural disasters, from the Pacific tsunami, to hurricane-devastated New Orleans and then Galveston on the US Gulf Coast, to the recent earthquake in Haiti. In such images we find ourselves not in the 'desert of the Real',[2] stripped of our humanist myths of progress and technological triumph, but upon the beachhead of Reality awaiting Ulysses' return.

For four years, work in the Last Resorts design research studio at the Rice School of Architecture has attempted to map this littoral, approaching design as the figuration of alternative dynamic processes between natural forces, cultural values and economic figures. Working with coastal engineers and geologist John Anderson, the case study has been Galveston Island, Texas, once one of the most important ports in North America and referred to as the 'Wall Street of the South'. The city of Galveston occupies a barrier island and was erased by a hurricane in 1900. This is still the greatest loss of life due to a natural disaster in US history. In 2008, Hurricane Ike devastated the island, exacerbating the already extreme coastal erosion that will only worsen due to rising sea levels in the coming decades.

Nkiru Mokwe and Viktor Ramos, Energe(ne)tic Fields, Last Resorts Studio, 2007

below: The proliferation and patterning of a buoyant structural component allows the design of a floating mega-structural community at the western terminus of the Galveston sea wall/Gulf of Mexico. Various configurations allow the system to stiffen to provide opportunities for habitation, or to flex to respond to wave energy and produce localised beaches and pockets of leisure.

opposite: One assemblage of the system configures a rigid spine of roads and inhabitable modules that transition into a more flexible structure with various skinning strategies to respond to localised experiential programmes.

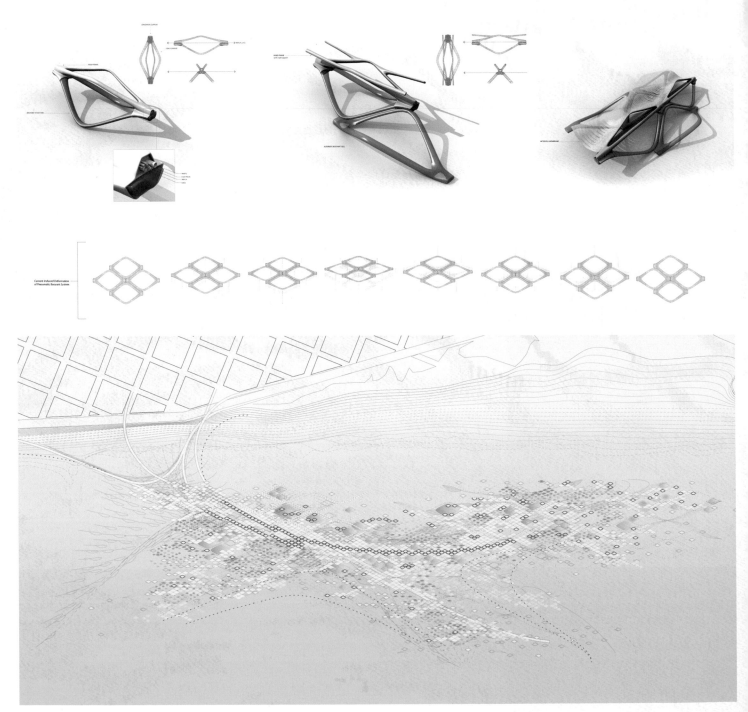

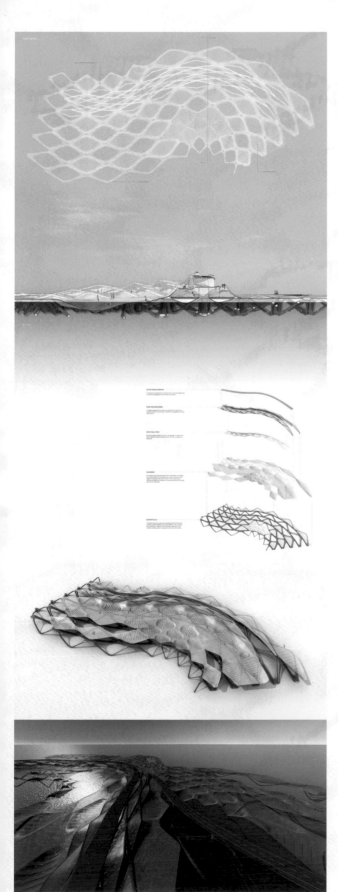

After the 1900 storm, the city was heroically rebuilt with an epochal sea wall that allowed it to exist for a hundred years in a post-*histoire* eddy. However it never recovered economically as the port and petrochemical industry were relocated to the port of Houston (made possible by an equally stunning feat of engineering hubris: the dredging of a ship channel more than 48 kilometres/30 miles long). Today, Galveston is a centre of historical preservation, cruise shipping and numerous events each year that bolster its tourism industry (such as December's 'Dickens on the Strand' in which tourists don frock coats to simulate *A Christmas Carol* past that David Copperfield would not recognise). Populations along the Gulf of Mexico have grown rapidly due to low capital costs, the North American Free Trade Association (NAFTA), and the linking of established petrochemicals hubs along the US Gulf Coast with the development of South America's energy reserves. The area is one of the world's hubs of oil refining and shipping, and the island itself was recently booming as the last reasonably priced developable coastal real-estate in North America.

Now, after Hurricane Ike, little long-range planning has occurred for the city's future, because to do so requires reconceptualising the material relationship between city and sea, and through it the humanist division between culture and nature. The sea wall conceptually and quite literally serves as an infrastructural line that delineates natural forces from human orders. It is now at the end of its life and will require significant refurbishment and extension. In their Energe(ne)tic Fields project, Rice students Nkiru Mokwe and Viktor Ramos developed a buoyant structural component that proliferated into performative assemblages. These allow opportunities for habitation or flexible membranes to respond to wave energy, beaches and pockets of leisure. One assemblage of the system configures a rigid spine of roads and inhabitable modules that transition into a more flexible structure with various skinning strategies that in turn respond to localised experiential programmes. The simple line of the existing sea wall and its modern dichotomies of nature versus culture are delaminated, modulated, and otherwise transformed into a complex territory that suggests entanglements of nature-cultures.

In a broader sense, we understand the line of the sea wall as merely the largest example of infrastructures and processes, such as the ship-lane dredging, jetties and land 'reclamation' that characterise the Gulf Coast, and which now determine its ecosystem. New islands of dredged material produce habitats for the fauna that drive ecotourism. Like attempts to reconstruct a Victorian past that never existed, such artificial landscapes can be understood as 'restoration' projects in that they attempt to return the bay to at least elements of its preindustrial – its

**North Keeragool and Kathryn Pakenham,
Fluctuating Territories, Last Resorts Studio, Rice
School of Architecture, Houston, Texas, 2008**
Fluctuating Territories, turning attention from the
beachside to the Galveston Bay edge, seeks to
activate the relationship with the mainland through
a network of ecotourism, leisure sites, fishing and
birding. A phased strategy identifies immediate
opportunities on particular sites and builds upon
them in time to produce a cohesive network that
integrates the underutilised back of the island and
converts it into a economically and ecologically
productive environment.

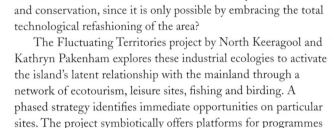

The project symbiotically offers platforms for programmes while constructing new wetlands. Over time, such nodes are linked to produce a network integrating the underutilised Galveston Bay into an economically and ecologically productive environment.

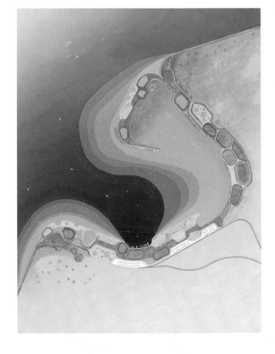

natural – state. But what is at stake in the fantasy of restoration and conservation, since it is only possible by embracing the total technological refashioning of the area?

The Fluctuating Territories project by North Keeragool and Kathryn Pakenham explores these industrial ecologies to activate the island's latent relationship with the mainland through a network of ecotourism, leisure sites, fishing and birding. A phased strategy identifies immediate opportunities on particular sites. The project symbiotically offers platforms for programmes while constructing new wetlands. Over time, such nodes are linked to produce a network integrating the under-utilised Galveston Bay into an economically and ecologically productive environment. This effectively reorients the coastal region's identity from isolated beach resorts and petrochemical plants to an ecocentred community.

Another project, Urban Corrugations by Johnny Chen and Elizabeth Mickey, explores the potential to inhabit one of the largest dredge deposit sites behind the sea wall. It is also one of the largest and most disaster-resistant empty sites in the area, suggesting the potential to relocate the centroid of density. The design blurs landscape and building through an intensive strategy of dredged berms deployed as a new topography. The high-density development produces natural and cultural amenities as well as diverse atmospheres of water and wetlands to foster mutuality between human occupation and natural systems.

In contrast, the All Tomorrow's Parties project by Alberto Govela and Asma Husain exudes a dystopic vision. Under the worst case, by 2058 sea-level rise and increased hurricane activity due to global climate change may render the US Gulf Coast unstable and in some cases uninhabitable. Meanwhile, the offshore oil and gas platforms could become attractive sites for offshore wind and wave farms while providing artificial reefs. The project suggests that the shallow warm waters of the Gulf could become a centre for the recovery of world fish stocks and a gastro- and ecotourism magnet. Just as the oil companies became land developers for the first suburban master-planned communities, completing a petrochemicals-fuelled loop of consumption and production into a lifestyle, these platforms here become hosts for an offshore leisure society housed in a gigantic space-frame that bridges the reused platforms. While the rest of the world endures ongoing energy rationing, the inhabitants gorge themselves on the local surplus of free electricity as the super-wealthy and post-oil nomads mingle outside any state or federal jurisdiction. Whether one sees this steam-punk as an image of benign emergence or a manifestation of 'shock doctrine',[3] such designs serve not as a projection of the future so much as incisions into the potentials of our present existential condition through design.

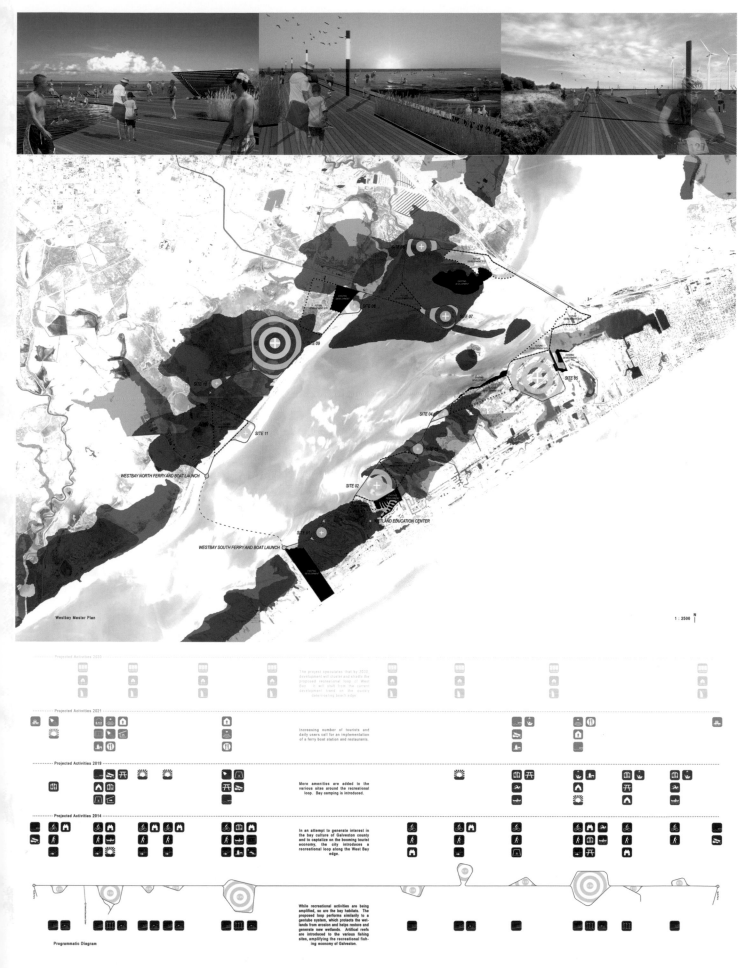

Westbay Master Plan

WESTBAY NORTH FERRY AND BOAT LAUNCH

WESTBAY SOUTH FERRY AND BOAT LAUNCH

WETLAND EDUCATION CENTER

1 : 2500

Projected Activities 2030

The project speculates that by 2030, development will cluster and circle the proposed recreational loop of West Bay. It will shift from the current development trend on the gulf's deteriorating beach edge.

Projected Activities 2021

Increasing number of tourists and daily users call for an implementation of a ferry boat station and restaurants.

Projected Activities 2019

More amenities are added to the various sites around the recreational loop. Bay camping is introduced.

Projected Activities 2014

In an attempt to generate interest in the bay culture of Galveston county and to capitalize on the booming tourist economy, the city introduces a recreational loop along the West Bay edge.

While recreational activities are being amplified, so are the bay habitats. The proposed loop performs similarity to a geotube system, which protects the wetlands from erosion and helps restore and generate new wetlands. Artificial reefs are introduced to the various fishing sites, amplifying the recreational fishing economy of Galveston.

Programmatic Diagram

83

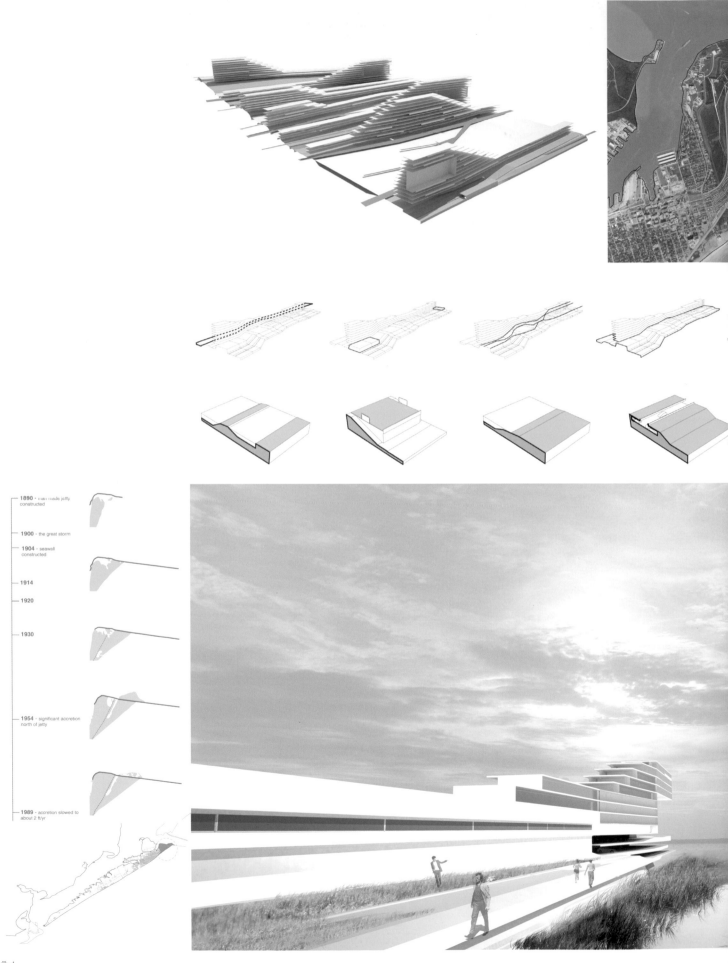

1890 - man made jetty constructed

1900 - the great storm

1904 - seawall constructed

1914

1920

1930

1954 - significant accretion north of jetty

1989 - accretion slowed to about 2 ft/yr

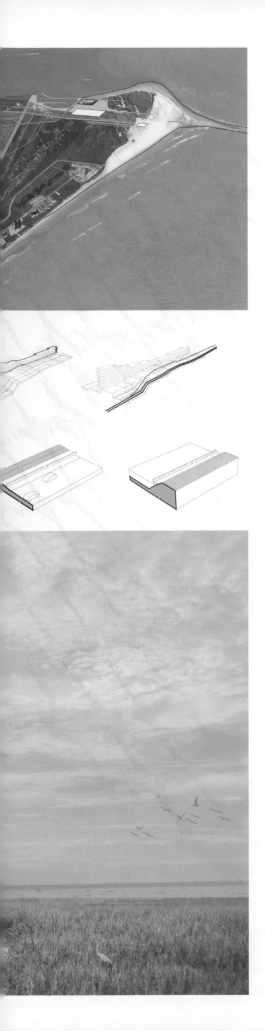

Michel Foucault's closing of *The Order of Things* (1970) described the modern humanist subject being washed away, like a figure in the sand, by the incoming tide of history, to be replaced by new inscriptions of knowledge. This projection now seems all too literal.[4] Giorgio Agamben has argued that modern knowledge, power and politics have revolved around the dialectical relationship of the closed human world (a world of representations, cultural constructions and technical extensions) to the open one of inhuman nature (an earth of forces, matter, operations and animal intensities).[5] Beginning in the late 18th century, this dialectic was concretised and territorialised as the spaces and forms of the metropolis. Thus the modern city was not simply the site where blasé subjects of industrialisation were fashioned, but where a modern epistemological drama between the human and inhuman played out most spectacularly.

In tracking a shift away from such humanist topographies, Bruno Latour has suggested that the legitimating function of the natural, an at once transcendental and distant shore upon which humanist thought has always run aground, must be replaced by new sites, forms and spaces of political ecology. For him, the significance of modernity is not the often lamented alienation of culture from nature, but rather the proliferation of phenomena, things, devices and experiences that refuse to fall under either category and instead produce hybrid mixtures of nature-cultures.[6] If Foucault's figure of man is swept away with the tide and replaced with entanglements between nature and cultures, the sites where new configurations will be manifested may very well be those where the relationship between patterns of cultural life and natural forces are most in conflict and yet most enticing. Just as Galveston became a glowing after-image of the polis in the 20th century, it may be a harbinger of the political ecologies for this one. ∆

Notes

1. See http://marineeconomics.noaa.gov/socioeconomics/assessment/population.html.
2. Jean Baudrillard, 'Simulacra and simulation', in Mark Poster (ed), *Jean Baudrillard: Selected Writings*, Stanford University Press (Stanford, CA), 1988, pp 166–84.
3. Naomi Klein, *The Shock Doctrine*, Picador (New York), 2008.
4. Michel Foucault, *The Order of Things: An Archaeology of the Human Sciences*, Tavistock (London), 1970.
5. Giorgio Agamben, *The Open: Man and Animal*, Stanford University Press (Stanford, CA), 2004.
6. Bruno Latour, *We Have Never Been Modern*, Harvard University Press, 1993; Latour, *Politics of Nature: How to Bring the Sciences into Democracy*, Harvard University Press, 2004.

Anthony Burke

**Melissa Petrovic, Bays Precinct Masterplan Study,
Computational Media Masters Studio (tutors: Anthony Burke
and Ben Hewett), University of Technology, Sydney, 2009**
Single computational regimes tend towards homogenous design
spaces. In this example, multiple systems are used in sequence
to avoid totalising geometries, developing intelligence through
time that deals with multiple scales and constraints.

THE URBAN COMPLEX
SCALAR PROBABILITIES AND URBAN COMPUTATION

Guest-editor **Anthony Burke** redefines complexity in relation to the city as 'a dynamic and luminal organisational condition "growing at the edge of chaos"' and in so doing shifts our understanding of urban trauma as an event intrinsic to the contribution of the metropolis rather than external to it.

Cities are intrinsically complex. Attempts to model, understand and ultimately shape these complex systems has been of intense interest to architects and urban planners since the 1950s, taking on a new urgency in light of the massive urban changes and projects being developed in the emerging economies of the world. The often quoted statistic that the planet is now more urban than rural has lent force to the intensity of this focus, having the masters studios of the architectural academies scrambling to all corners of the world, motivating practices to internationalise and capitalise on the new gold rush, and refocusing new technologies in design on the question of urbanism and the city. So after 50 years or more of urban computation, why has the urban condition remained so resistant to attempts to parametricise its inherent complexity? Put another way, why have the assumptions of urban systems models proven to be incompatible with the reality of the contemporary urban condition, and incapable of accommodating or recognising contemporary events and behaviours?

The commonly understood meaning of complexity is to have many elements within a situation: this is complexity based on quantity. A complex is also understood in psychology as a set of connected mental factors, a node in the unconscious of emotional responses that are associated, knowingly or not, by the individual with a particular subject or recognisable theme resulting in a set of habituated responses to a circumstance; that is, a *sub*liminal organisational condition structuring behaviour. It is arguable that current approaches to the computational modelling of the urban environment have these same qualities. They deal primarily with quantity and its distribution, and replay habitual response to urban systems logics entrenched through the cybernetics of mid-last century. They have developed relatively unchallenged into the contemporary parametric computational systems being used for urban design today.

Complexity as a science, however, refers to the behaviour of a system, focusing on its dynamic qualities and the assumption of systemic instability or dynamic poise. In particular, complexity as a lens through which to understand the city undermines the assumptions of hierarchically parametric computational orders, and restates the fundamental complexity of the city as a dynamic and liminal organisational condition 'growing at-the-edge of chaos',[1] an environment where organisation is continually being brought into being.

If we understand complexity and its relationship to the urban in this way, a new series of logics dominate the discussion. These are based on the dynamic poise and potential for chaotic and overly ordered states (catastrophes) inherent in systems far from equilibrium. In this context, trauma as an event and its effects are not external to a system, but intrinsically constitutive of a city's ongoing organisational becoming.[2] Trauma as an event is ontologically constitutive of self-organising critical systems. In recognising this, how does the issue of urban trauma, as a product of liminal dynamic organisational structures, create a space for critical reflection that has largely been lacking in digital urban systems discourse?

Before it is possible to continue with this line of reasoning, however, it is necessary to understand the relation between trauma and complexity more precisely. Trauma is associated with an event as the rupture between expected and experienced behaviour. Whether it be war, environmental catastrophe, economic sanctions or global warming, trauma is the result of an experience of the unexpected or the statistically improbable, an occurrence that is beyond the habitual frame of normal behaviour and incapable of being accommodated within a (moral, computational) system without a form of systemic adjustment.

Complexity science has explored natural events such as earthquakes, volcanic eruptions, epileptic seizures and market crashes that display the properties of what Per Bak calls adaptive 'self-organising criticality'.[3] He describes this as 'the tendency of large systems with many components to evolve into a poised, "critical state", way out of balance, where minor disturbances may lead to events, called avalanches, of all sizes.' He goes on to write: 'The state is established solely because of the dynamical interaction among individual elements of the system: the critical state is self-organized.'[4] It is this condition of self-organising criticality intrinsic to complex systems like cities, and their capacity to internally generate avalanches towards an improbable system state, that forms the conditions under which trauma is created and perpetuated.

During a decade of process-oriented research in digital techniques and technologies, the city has been tested by a battery of technological procedures and analogies. These have maintained the belief that an accurate simulation of the behaviour of an urban condition is possible through the deconstruction of urban systems into their constitutive layers. The more layers, the more integrated the model, and the more predictable its performance, the better. Richard Garber summarises this prevalent view, writing: 'The potential of building information modeling (BIM) is that a single, intelligent, virtual model can be used to satisfy all aspects of the design process.'[5] The assumption here is that the perfect model is required to integrate all information pertinent to a project, and respond in a predictable way, simultaneously stabilising the probability of all moments of negotiation and tension within a design framework.

Traumatic possibility critiques this assumption, recognising the movement of a system's behaviour from high to low probability states (scales of probability) as consistent with a coherent yet open logical model, and an effect of the poised critical balance inherent in complex dynamic systems such as cities. A complex urban system should actually generate new organisational possibilities through its systemic structure and behavioural dynamics. It is unstable in this sense, but inclusive of not only information that is at hand, but

generative of new information which is intrinsic to the system itself. It is this capacity of a complex system to continually adjust its poise and explore its range of probable states that causes it to continually self-organise into new forms of coherence that foreshadows the ongoing possibility of a large-scale system event, and systemically establishes and perpetuates the presence of the traumatic.

Urban Dynamics and the Formation of the Urban Complex

If we accept the condition of the traumatic as part of a complex but fundamental urban dynamic, the limits of current geometry-focused atemporal parametric approaches to urban modelling quickly become evident. Recent parametric urban experiments, and the proclamation of parametricism as a new style, if anything, have shown signs of exhaustion after a very brief period, as the incompatibility of the hierarchical systems logic and the urban have become clearly irreconcilable. Given Jay Forrester's Urban Dynamics experiments and their failure to predicatively or operationally impact on the city in the 1960s, this should not be surprising, as the underlying logic of parametric urban experimentation today is exactly the same, to the point of using common representational systems to visualise the relationships. The assumptions of stability (homeostasis) founded in early systems master-planning approaches were sublimated during the early 1960s when computational approaches to urbanism moved from the data collection and analysis of Constantinos Doxiadis' Ekistics research, for example, to the solution-engineering approach of Forrester. Contemporary parametric software (building information modelling and city information modelling) systems are only the latest technology upgrade to entrench these essentially conservative cybernetic logics of organisation in design. They have remained largely beyond critique in urban terms and rarely challenged from a systems point of view.

What this points to is the current tension in the discourse on computational design in architecture between the vitality of an information-rich unpredictability, and new orders of optimisation and systemic control. To propose that one system can do all – design, integrate and optimize – is to misunderstand the needs of the design phase against the needs of a procurement phase within the different scales and cycles of architectural and urban production. While geometry-based urban propositions enable the control of many relationships in the name of an idealised predictability, the post-traumatic condition simply refuses that form of stability as a meaningful urban condition, raising the need to reconsider fundamental assumptions of the digitally understood city.

Currently in avant-garde design, complexity has become a visual signature that is easily reproduced, confusing masses of data and its display with the nature of real information. At

Complexity science has explored natural events such as earthquakes, volcanic eruptions, epileptic seizures and market crashes that display the properties of what Per Bak calls adaptive 'self-organising criticality'.

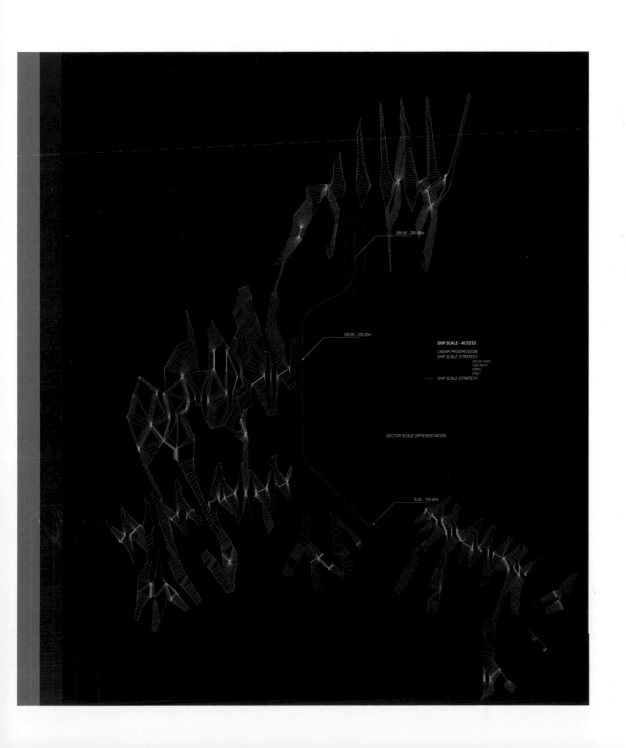

Ben Yee, Bays Precinct Masterplan Study, Computational
Media Masters Studio, University of Technology, Sydney, 2009
Using scripts capable of significant scalar modularity, this
diagram study of the Bays Precinct master plan in Sydney
Harbour focused on scripted techniques that developed a
large range of scales of response to seed site conditions and
their development towards a highly articulated mega-structural
framework. Establishing a regime of multiple scales and
layered scripted responses begins to overcome the hegemony
of computational integration in favour of a more radically
responsive and complex urban position.

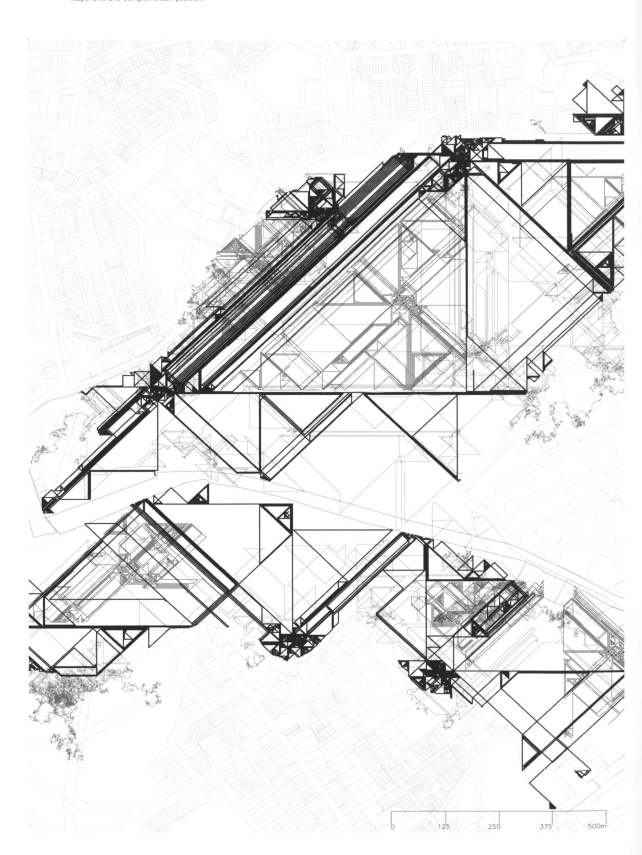

0   125   250   375   500m

its worst, blankets of smothering white geometry proliferate without sense or intention across huge swathes of London or Mumbai, calcifying urban life in the name of advanced design. Computational systems become severed from their relation to complex and changing underlying urban environments in favour of formal continuity without meaningful resistance or tension; that is, without relevance.

Information and Probability

The post-traumatic condition is that potent environment in which fundamental reorganisation is possible. In its negative form, this is the moment of Naomi Klein's 'disaster capitalism',[6] a vacuum in which no controlling mechanism operates, providing an opportunity for predatory systems to dominate. But it is also one in which the mechanisms of a system's resilience are exposed.

In its most stark form, the reality of the traumatic event in shaping urban form and development challenges the basic assumption that any system created to forecast or design stable urban behaviour can reconcile a meaningful grouping of intrinsic logics with the effects of unpredictable (very low probability) forces at the limits of a system's state-space. However, it is the site of a system's informational limits that links two key terms – 'information' and 'probability' – that become key concepts within a complex urban systems logic.

In this sense, the post-traumatic is an information-rich environment, given that: 'Information … is inversely proportional to probability: the more probable, the less information, the less probable, the more information.'[7] If we consider the link between information and complexity, the parametricist taboo of 'unmediated juxtapositions'[8] denies precisely the possibility of an information-rich space. In this sense, parametric systems tend towards the side of stability, self-regulation and balance, a minimal information state.

The traumatic event, then, can be understood as part of every complex system-space including the urban, existing in the long tail of probability, topologically consistent although proportionally exceptional and temporally very rare. Perhaps it is more useful to understand trauma and its production through these rare events as the enduring echo of a change in a system's level of complexity or information quotient, where a system is wrenched from its probabilistically normal range of behaviour towards a new degree of complexity. This is the moment when information is produced, also producing the traumatic echo through attempts to reconcile new information into a dynamically 'poised' system.

What this highlights is the recognition that to develop conceptual models for urban environments is to acknowledge, as Galloway and Thacker do, the contemporary 'experience of systematicity itself, of an integration of

technology, biology and politics'.[9] It challenges the distinctions between politics and technology that dominate discussions of the city, and begins to frame a theoretical apparatus capable of bringing these narratives together.

How, then, is it useful to think about urban design models and their contemporary technological apparatus in light of the post-traumatic condition? Can the space of the post-traumatic (slow or fast) be productively harnessed in design terms? Would not this require a far more judicious use of computational systems in architecture and urban design, one that seeks to incorporate a dynamic sense of probability into its framework to produce productive differences between system-states? Can we consider the discontinuous as at least as important as the formal sense of continuity delivered by the parametric proposals we are already so used to seeing?

What the post-traumatic requires us to consider in design terms is how we work with a range of systems logics at the limits of order and chaos. These are of a different conceptual type to the parametric apparatus appropriate at an architectural level; different scales have their own problems. Engaging with complexity as a foundation for rebuilding urban systems modelling refuses stability and minimal information states, and establishes design opportunity through the concept of a continuously generative urban dynamic, seeking a vitality in urban thinking that is absent from questions of geometry alone. ∆

Notes
1. Michael Batty, *Cities and Complexity: Understanding Cities with Cellular Automata, Agent-Based Models, and Fractals*, MIT Press (Cambridge, MA), 2005, p 478.
2. See Andrew Benjamin, 'Trauma Within the Walls: Notes Towards a Philosophy of the City' on pp 24–31 of this issue.
3. The concept of self-organising criticality is attributed to Per Bak, and used to understand rare macroscopic events such as earthquakes as a build-up of small earthquakes that don't stop. *Self-organizing criticality* is unpredictable. *Intermittent criticality* is an accumulation of amplifying cascades that does offer the possibility of prediction. This class of catastrophic event includes stock-market crashes and epileptic seizure. Érdi argues that: 'Complex behavior in nature reflects the tendency of large systems with many components to evolve into a poised "critical state", way out of balance, where minor disturbances may lead to events, called avalanches, of all sizes.' See Péter Érdi, *Complexity Explained*, Springer (Berlin), 2008, p 329.
4. Per Bak as quoted in Péter Érdi, op cit, p 329.
5. Richard Garber, 'Optimisation Stories: The Impact of Building Information Modelling on Contemporary Design Practice', in ∆ *Closing the Gap: Information Models in Contemporary Design Practice*, Vol 79, No 2, 2009, p 8.
6. Naomi Klein, *The Shock Doctrine: The Rise of Disaster Capitalism*, Metropolitan Books (New York), 2008.
7. Mark C Taylor, *The Moment of Complexity*, University of Chicago Press (Chicago, IL), 2001, p 109.
8. Patrik Schumacher, 'Parametricism: A New Global Style for Architecture and Urban Design', in ∆ *Digital Cities*, Vol 79, No 4, 2009, p 20.
9. Alexander R Galloway and Eugene Thacker, *The Exploit: A Theory of Networks*, University of Minnesota Press (Minneapolis, MN), 2007, p 70.

PROJECT FOR A MEDITERRANEAN UNION

President Sarkozy's proposal in 2008 for a
Mediterranean Union connected by a high-speed
rail link prompted a series of speculative projects by
Masters students at the University of Technology,
Sydney. **Adrian Lahoud** asks how the cultural,
economic and political world would shift if we
could catch a train from Beirut to Tel Aviv.

Martin Abbott, Georgia Herbert, Clare Johnston, Joshua Lynch and Alexandra Wright, The Diversity Machine and the Resilient Network, Beirut, Social Transformations Studio (tutors: Adrian Lahoud and Samantha Spurr), University of Technology, Sydney, 2009
The project proposes a layered strategy whereby a strict horizontal datum is established at the ground and roof plane. The programme activates a variable bandwidth through the middle of the fabric.

inset: New vectors for growth extend across the water's edge forming armatures and scaffolding for future expansion.

On 13 July 2008, French President Nicolas Sarkozy proposed a plan for the creation of a union made up of the all the littoral nations of the Mediterranean.[1] A key part of this proposal would be the creation of a high-speed rail (HSR) line running along the shore of the Mediterranean Basin and linking the Maghreb and the Levant to the coast of the Aegean, the Balkans, Southern Europe and the Iberian Peninsula. This single loop of infrastructure spanning from Gibraltar to the Bosporus would take in 21 separate states, four time zones and seven major seas, and connect the continents of Africa, Asia and Europe. The combined population of the littoral states is half a billion people.

Infrastructural Conflict
During the Lebanese Civil War in Beirut between 1975 until the Taif Accord in 1990, a great fissure opened across the city, swallowing all signs of life. Under the panoptic gaze of concrete hulks – like the towering unfinished Holiday Inn – sniper fire and shelling methodically carved uninhabitable chunks from the heart of the city. Civilisation retreated from its precipice, taking with it almost all commerce and human traffic, and leaving in its wake a post-apocalyptic exclusion zone. Eventually, through the pockmarked masonry of Beirut's Ottoman colonnades, among its piles of burnt-out cars and open sewers, nature returned to reclaim its place in the city, and the fissure of urban ruination that eventually came to hold apart this city for 15 years turned deep green with plant life.

In underdeveloped Sudan, some 400 kilometres (248 miles) north of Khartoum, is a modern stretch of highway linking the village of Almatig to the Sudanese capital. This impressive piece of infrastructure was mainly completed using heavy earth-moving equipment that had previously been put to use boring tunnels – tunnels to hide Mujahidin fighters in the mountainous landscape of Afghanistan during the Soviet invasion. When the road was completed in 1993, its Saudi construction engineer and developer was not yet widely known outside of the US State Department and the circles of Afghani resistance. In 2001 he would orchestrate the most decisive terrorist attack in history.[2]

Standing between the old Green Line that once partitioned Lebanon's capital, and Osama Bin Laden's 800-kilometre (497-mile) highway to Khartoum, is a shattered landscape littered by all the remnants of political dysfunction and human frustration. It is a zone manned by checkpoints, divided by impermeable barriers and protected by blast walls – it is torn apart by maps and settlements and the extreme disparities of development. From Dahiyeh to the Golan, from Tel Aviv to Haifa, Hebron and Gaza, lies a comprehensive spatial catalogue of exceptions, breaks, ruptures and interruptions, as countless actors struggle over formation and destruction of the infrastructure networks that sustain life.

There is an inexhaustible contingency in the object or artefact since it is always caught up in relations with the other objects on which it depends. It is here that a breach was detected, the smallest of openings with which to sever some old alliances and begin the speculative project of imagining new forms of infrastructure for a Mediterranean Union.

This zone of conflict borders a sea whose currents are fuelled by differentials of pressure between north and south, by an excess of desire and a deficit of opportunity. The short stretches of sea between Tunisia and Lampudesa and between Morocco and Spain are the most heavily policed in the world, filled with the migratory flows of refugee boats, coastguards, fishing trawlers and drug traffickers.

In this context, how do we locate Sarkozy's proposal?

One might easily reduce the idea of Mediterranean Union (MU) to a series of geopolitical stratagems. It might emerge out of a strategic jostling between France and its neighbour Germany. Perhaps it is a competition to secure resource transport corridors between Russia, the Persian Gulf, Central Asia and the European Union. It might be the beginning of a renewed engagement with Africa as a site of agricultural production and labour that follows on similar interest from China and the Gulf states. Despite all these likelihoods, there is an unintended payload aboard the announcement, a secret latency that has hitched a ride. Infrastructure is irreducible to its ideological origin.[3] There is an inexhaustible contingency in the object or artefact since it is always caught up of relations with the other objects on which it depends. It is here that a breach was detected, the smallest of openings with which to sever some old alliances and begin the speculative project of imagining new forms of infrastructure for a Mediterranean Union.

Speculative Objects

What if we simply refuse to inherit the type of discourse that characterises all argument about the region, a discourse plagued by road maps, peace plans, initiatives, deadlocks and frustrations? Can we find a vulnerable flank and establish a new conversation outside of this discursive space?[4] Can we simply posit – by sheer speculative force – another space of possibility? This leads to a disarming question: what if we could catch a train from Beirut to Tel Aviv?

The question animated a series of speculative proposals by Master of Architecture students at the University of Technology, Sydney for a new MU HSR and associated infrastructure in the Lebanese capital of Beirut. The site for the project is the extension to the Beirut Central District, a piece of reclaimed land created during the civil war. During the war, only half the city had access to waste disposal; the other half dumped rubbish at sea creating a large mound on the coast. Then, in 1990, the exhumed remains of war, excess building material and rubble generated by the reconstruction project, were added to the pile. Architecture as landfill for more architecture.

The Diversity Machine and Resilient Network (by students Martin Abbott, Georgia Herbert, Clare Johnston, Joshua Lynch and Alexandra Wright) begins with the idea that Beirut's existing urban fabric is highly decentralised because of the impact of conflict. The immobility imposed by a divided city and 15 years of civil war led to the development of a patchwork of small neighbourhoods that are relatively autonomous with regards to the provision of most of the social infrastructure necessary for daily life.

below left: Abu Dhabi Airport, United Arab Emirates, 2009. Just as the United Arab Emirates emerges as a staging point between Asia and Europe because of air travel, high-speed rail could turn Beirut into a hub city linking European and Middle Eastern networks.

below right: Speculative departures board, Beirut high-speed rail station, Lebanon, 2009. The possibility of these names appearing in sequence animates the project.

bottom: Tida Tippapart, Palestine, 2010. An elevated settler road, the town of Beit Jala connects Jerusalem with the outlying settlement outposts within the Palestinian West Bank. A vast network of infrastructure connects Israeli settlements and severs Palestinian territory, forcing Palestinians to take alternative routes winding below the exclusively Israeli roads.

Existing Distribution of Infrastructure across Mediterranean Union

Proposed High Speed Rail Loop

Potential Tertiary Rail Infrastructure

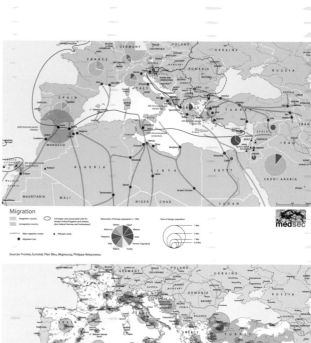

Migration

Sources: Frontex, Eurostat, Plan Bleu, Migreurop, Philippe Rekacewicz

Population

Population in urban centre
(Estimation where data not available)

Sources: Center for International Earth Science Information
Network (CIESIN), Columbia University; World Gazetteer

Non-renewable Natural Resources

Sources: Russian Energy Atlas, Swiss World Atlas, Plan Bleu,
www.nabucco-pipeline.com, Energy Tribune

Water

Sources: Plan Bleu, Global Water Intelligence, Great Man Made River Authority, Philippe Rekacewicz

Erik Escalante and Alina McConnochie, Beirut City Extension: Imperfect Difference, Incomplete Repetition, Social Transformations Studio, University of Technology, Sydney, 2009
opposite left top: Existing rail infrastructure along the shoreline of the Mediterranean. The image shows the extreme north–south disparity of infrastructural rail investment. While southern Europe is a densely interconnected network, North Africa and the Middle East are empty.

opposite left middle: The proposed high-speed rail line forms a looping conduit across the broken infrastructural landscape of the Levant and northern Africa linking zones of intense social and economic inequality. The relationship between North Africa and southern Europe will become increasingly important in years to come due to intense pressure from the energy and tourism sectors. This is already leading to an increased relationship between the regions as old animosities give way to cooperation based on economic necessity.

opposite left bottom: The new loop along the shoreline becomes a staging point for infrastructural expansion through the depth of the territory by initiating growth of secondary and tertiary lines to regional centres.

Emmanuelle Bournay and Matthias Beilstein, Environment and Security issues in the Southern Mediterranean Region: Exploring and Mapping the Issues, Mediterranean, 2009
opposite right: The Mediterranean basin is bound by North Africa, the Middle East and southern Europe. The vastly different social and economic conditions in each of these regions charge the sea with unequal pressure. The sea conditions the traffic along the littoral and through the depth of the surrounding nations. New organisations such as Medsec have evolved to deal with these complex supraterritorial political assemblages.

below: The new Gulf Corporation Council (GCC) rail line that is currently under construction and the speculative Mediterranean Union high-speed rail line form twin loops of mobility with the city of Beirut poised at their nexus. Can rail travel be to Beirut what air travel has been to the Gulf?

The instability of war has led to the development of an urban fabric that is able to reorganise itself around disruptions – the city has absorbed the DNA of conflict into its material organisation.

Lebanon and Region

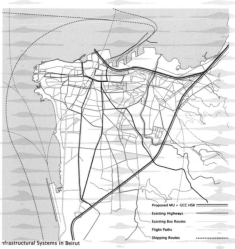

Proposed MU + GCC HSR
Existing Highways
Existing Bus Routes
Flight Paths
Shipping Routes

Infrastructural Systems in Beirut

The result of this organisation is an urban fabric that lacks consolidation and that (from the point of view of Modernist planning) lacks optimisation or efficiency. Rather than see this as a weakness, however, the project argues that it is precisely the 'redundancy' of the distributed social infrastructure and relative autonomy of the neighbourhoods that lends the city its resilience. The instability of war has led to the development of an urban fabric that is able to reorganise itself around disruptions – the city has absorbed the DNA of conflict into its material organisation.

The second example from the Social Transformations Studio is a project for a high-density extension to the city by Erik Escalante and Alina McConnochie. In Beirut City Extension: Imperfect Difference, Incomplete Repetition, they argue that much of the recent development in the Middle East is caught between excessive difference and excessive repetition. The spectacle of emblematic towers jostling for attention in Dubai makes any individual variation entirely superficial and thus unrecognisable. When it becomes the motivating force behind design, 'individuality' destroys the possibility of difference as such. Conversely, in the mere repetition of traditional fabric we face the opposite problem, a system that is not pliable enough to cope with the demands of high-density living or modern public transport infrastructure. Is there something possible in the space between both these models?

The project asks: What if the manipulation of the climate in the public sphere was used to drive the formation of the building envelope from the outside in?

Erik Escalante and Alina McConnochie, Beirut City Extension: Imperfect Difference, Incomplete Repetition, Social Transformations Studio, University of Technology, Sydney, 2009
above: This high-density, high-performance building fabric extends out from the existing city edge where it intersects with a modulated surface which deforms to accommodate the infrastructure network's requirements.

opposite: The urban interior of the proposed high-speed railway station is shaped by the envelopes of the clustered towers that enclose the platform.

Erik Escalante and Alina McConnochie,
Beirut City Extension: Imperfect
Difference, Incomplete Repetition, Social
Transformations Studio, University of
Technology, Sydney, 2009
opposite bottom: The clusters of larger
types clearly group around the different
transport nodes forming shaded public
interiors at the ground level. Also visible
are the distinct typological families that
nest around each of the transport nodes.

opposite top: Beirut, Lebanon, 2009.
This waste site has been compacted and
cleared ready for the construction of the
planned Beirut financial district. This piece
of reclaimed land, owned by the private
development company Solidere, formed the
site for the speculated HSR station.

Functioning like a conveyor at the scale of continents, the proposal for an HSR line around the shore of the Mediterranean would warp the space–time fabric of an entire region.

The project sets out to develop sets of related mini-tower typologies that group and nest in collective clusters. These clusters are organised around larger tower types that are in turn arranged around transport nodes. The collective assemblages form a series of differentiated neighbourhoods based on the interdependence of mobility networks. The urban fabric and the network must therefore be considered as two intimately linked infrastructures that reciprocally determine each other. The project asks: What if the manipulation of the climate in the public sphere was used to drive the formation of the building envelope from the outside in? By responding to this question the students shift the terms of the sustainability debate away from an idea of individual insulation towards one of a collective and distributed climatological infrastructure. The stakes are nothing less than a new vision for urban development organised around collective typologies and high-performance urban fabric.

Strange Networks

Functioning like a conveyor at the scale of continents, the proposal for an HSR line around the shore of the Mediterranean would warp the space–time fabric of an entire region. Though it might just be another vector of colonial expansion into a resource-rich region – a tendril of influence extending like the old Ottoman rail lines or Roman *viae*, it would nonetheless link long disputed territories and as yet unformed nations, stringing together a seemingly impossible series of names: Gaza, Barcelona, Beirut, Haifa, Tel Aviv, Cairo, and a much longer list of improbable actors including, but not limited to, Hassan Nasrallah, rail gauges,

water tables, Palestinian telecommunications networks, Saharan dust storms, reservoirs of aromatic hydrocarbons, re-insurers, risk analysts, refugees, ocean currents and alleged Iranian enrichment programmes. The role of a speculative object within this strange network is to catalyse the formation of new alliances around it and slowly, through much work and persuasion, to begin to form a territory that is an invitation to new friends and a provocation to unknown enemies. ⌂

Notes
1. BBC news, 13 July 2008. See http://news.bbc.co.uk/2/hi/7504214. stm, accessed 02 April 2010. Though the Mediterranean Union has been formally established with headquarters in Barcelona and a Jordanian, Ahmad Masa'deh, currently in charge, there has been very little in the way of concrete progress on any significant issues such as economic partnership, let alone sharing of infrastructure or co-development.
2. See Robert Fisk, 'Anti-Soviet Warrior Puts His Arm on the Road to Peace: The Saudi Businessman Who Recruited Mujahedin Now Uses them for Large-Scale Building Projects in Sudan', *The Independent*, 6 December 1993. See www.independent.co.uk/news/world/antisoviet-warrior-puts-his-army-on-the-road-to-peace-the-saudi-businessman-who-recruited-mujahedin-now-uses-them-for-largescale-building-projects-in-sudan-robert-fisk-met-him-in-almatig-1465715.html, accessed 2 April 2010.
3. See the interview with Slavoj Žižek on pages 110–15 of this issue.
4. Whoever decides on the framework for contest has won already. If we focus on the Middle East in particular, there is a conflict over a group of terms: 'terror, resistance, natural growth, expansion, proportionality.' Strategic advantage (and at some stage victory) depends on a struggle over the meaning of each term and its capacity to strengthen one's position vis-à-vis the enemy. These limits mark out the discursive space of the conflict. The tacit agreement that these terms and not some others outline the framework of the argument and thus the stakes for the negotiation is dependent on there being a disagreement as to the exact meaning of the individual terms themselves.

Caracas Sangrante, Caracas, 1994
above: Caracas Sangrante means, literally,
'Bleeding Caracas'. Nelson Garrido's
interventionist photography preceded a
sudden awareness of the current violent
situation within Venezuelan society that
has been explored more deeply in the
country's contemporary art.

Primer Plano de Caracas, Caracas, 1578
opposite: The earliest known map of
Caracas shows a schematic understanding
of its geography. Framed by roughly drafted
mountains, the grid starts following the
directions suggested by the Río Guaire and
its affluents.

FEARSCAPES: CARACAS
POSTCARDS FROM A VIOLENT CITY

Venezuelan architect, artist and educator **Eduardo Kairuz** reveals how beneath the stereotypical view of Caracas as the 'Murder Capital of the World' lies a history of savage imposition, dating back to its founding in the 16th century and its colonial past and manifested today in the stark social segregation between parts of the city.

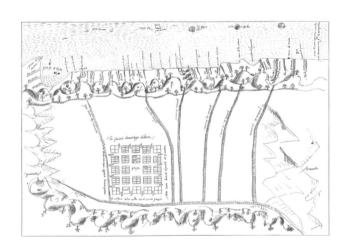

Plaza Bolívar, Caracas, c 1900
below: A Plaza Bolívar can be found in
every city, town and village in Venezuela.
Celebrating the figure of the heroic warrior
Simón Bolívar – an almost religious icon
known as 'the Liberator' and 'the Father of
the Homeland' – these spaces are usually
the epicentre of the urban fabric.

Unidad Residencial 2 de Diciembre,
Caracas, c 1960
opposite: Seen from above, Caracas
resembles a collage-like tapestry. Large and
populous precincts were arranged following
urban models inspired by cities such
as Paris, London and Madrid. Although
Unidad Residencial 2 de Diciembre (known
as 23 de Enero from January 1958) was
sited on a vast empty lot, it is another
urban model that contributes to the
distinctive discontinuous fabric of the city.

In September of 2009, *Foreign Policy* magazine placed Caracas, the capital of oil-rich Venezuela, as one of the most dangerous cities in the world, with an average of 96 violent deaths per 100,000 inhabitants.[1]

The city – a territory under siege by an intense climate of violence – had lost its previous grim title of 'Murder Capital of the World' to Ciudad Juárez, Mexico; another Latin American metropolis, a city ruled by drug cartels on the Mexico–US border and used to drug trafficking, extortion, express kidnapping and homicide.

Nevertheless – and despite this defeat – the spontaneous alterations to the city's architecture and urban structures triggered by the threats such forms of criminality have posed for Caracas' citizens are already having a devastating effect on its image.

But the violent disposition of Caracas is not new, nor does it manifest exclusively in its 'fearscape'.

The iconic images that follow prove that the conflicting nature of the city has always been there to contribute to a cityscape conditioned by disruption, isolation and a struggle for control.

Wounded Giants: Caracas Now
The decision to picture Caracas as a blood-drenched urban landscape, and to introduce it as such here, was not easy, for it seemed obvious, even biased. But the image (pp 101–02) shows an important piece of the city's architecture – one that represents power, vigour and ambition – as the victim of a brutal act of violence.

A repeatedly wounded landscape, it focuses on one of the symbols of Caracas' continuously unfulfilled promise of modernity: the heroic irruption of Parque Central. A highly dense city within the city developed in the late 1970s and comprising high-rise housing blocks, the highest office towers in South America and leisure, cultural and commercial facilities, this colossal structure is named after Central Park, New York City's largest open space.

This seemingly insignificant fact reveals the crisis of identity that Caracas has suffered over the years, and which is perhaps one of the aspects that has most influenced the configuration of the city's current fearscape.

Assault and Orthopaedics: Caracas circa 1580
Founded under the shadow of the abuse and genocide inflicted by European settlers on the indigenous communities that previously occupied the 'new territories', a violent and conflictive history can be traced throughout the development of the city.

In Caracas, briefly after seizing control of the valley in which it sits, Spanish settlers arranged the city by superimposing the grid, a recurrent mechanism of urban control enforced all over these territories.[2]

This mesh, whose emplacement in cities such as Bogotá, Mexico City and Buenos Aires produced unyielding urban structures, was an urban recipe that rarely took into account the cultural and geographical particularities of the settlements.

This imposition of an orthopaedic urban structure that could not foresee its own expansion within the particularities of its geography fostered the discontinuity we see in Caracas' current urban fabric.

Forced Identities: Caracas circa 1890

Previous to these discontinuities, at the end of the 19th century came the tension produced between imported urban models and the evolving conditions of the city.

It was at this time that an attempt was made to transform the deceptive postcard of a peaceful rural setting into an ambitious but nevertheless inconsistent plan for replicating Paris – the vision of General Antonio Guzmán Blanco, the country's first progressive autocrat and one of Venezuela's 'ruling strong men'.[3]

Among these historical political figures, it is paramount to mention General Marcos Pérez Jiménez, a dictator who ruled Venezuela from 1952 to 1958. He is remembered for his contribution to the rapid modernisation of the country, and the establishment of a fear society that was controlled through torture, imprisonment and forced disappearance.

Self-Assurance: Caracas circa 1950

However, under Pérez Jiménez's rule, the country – and Caracas in particular – would witness the most radical transformation it will ever see, as exemplified by the fast-track hyperscale development of Unidad 2 de Diciembre, known as 23 de Enero after the general was overthrown in 1958.

It was at this time that an attempt was made to transform the deceptive postcard of a peaceful rural setting into an ambitious but nevertheless inconsistent plan for replicating Paris.

This fragmented and yet continuous barrier not only limits the possibilities of embracing an urban culture of fluid continuity; it underlines opposing ideological beliefs that divide Venezuela's contemporary society.

This development, foremost among the plethora of modern interventions that were being developed all over the country at the time, occupies an area of 220 hectares (543.6 acres), and includes an array of social housing superblocks comprising more than 9,200 apartments and a series of complementary service buildings.

Built for more than 60,000 new city migrants in the relatively short period of only three years, this remarkable intervention was conceived by architect Carlos Raúl Villanueva under the ideals of Modern architecture and was realised thanks to the unprecedented wealth brought by oil revenues and Pérez Jiménez's ambition for Caracas to join the league of world-class modern cities.[4]

But these ruthless operations would also represent progress, as embodied in Modern architecture, by breaking up the grid, now considered a vestige of outdated urban models.

Viral Spontaneity: Caracas circa 1960

Yet no matter how remarkable the attempt at transforming Caracas into a truly modern city, there is the problem of containing the aggressive manifestation of informality.

The appearance of spontaneous urban settlements (a consequence of institutional inefficiency in coping with the continued demand for social housing and public services) is a non-centralised phenomenon that rapidly expanded to form the unplanned building accumulations commonly known as *barrios* – hyper-dense agglomerations of precarious dwellings lacking public space, services and regulations.

Usually situated in the peripheral areas of the city, the excluded settlements – distinctive for their labyrinthine

footpaths and intricate staircases – are the areas in which the highest rates of urban violence can be found. A product of a massive response to necessity, they define the current fearscape of the city, and have also been overexposed by local media as the only places in which crime, corruption and violence are manifested, and this has had an impact on the rest of the city's perception of these areas.

Fearscape: Caracas circa 2010

But reality has proved this wrong, as new embodiments of the wall – intended to contain the real and constructed threats of criminality – appear as yet another informal phenomenon of self-organisation that this time operates in the spaces occupied by the city's middle and upper classes.

An aggressive operation on the city's facade, the unplanned implementation of security devices such as walls, fences, barricades, shattered glass, electrified and barbed wire, watchtowers, surveillance cameras and gated community checkpoints (to name just a few) is applied to the existing architecture and urban structures, transgressing their integrity and triggering the emergence of episodes of spatial segregation and social disarticulation that characterise the city.

This fragmented and yet continuous barrier not only limits the possibilities of embracing an urban culture of fluid continuity; it underlines the opposing ideological beliefs that divide Venezuela's contemporary society.

Overcoming Trauma

It is reasonable to believe that a different outcome would have been impossible to achieve as hostility seems embedded within the DNA of this city.

It also seems obvious that in having to cope with the burden of a ruthless colonial past, independence gained through warfare, continuous overthrows of power and the imposed implementations of foreign identities, the current manifestations of violence were unavoidable.

But this conflictive quality – what appears to be the constitutive feature of the city – might be there just waiting to be embraced through unprejudiced and eager design strategies.

A first step might be to overcome a tradition of belief in miraculous remedies imposed by messianic institutions, individuals and ideologies.

Such an attitude might give way to a slow but steady transformation of the city, bringing progress and renovation alongside the inevitability of trauma; only this time in more manageable and acceptable levels. ∆

Notes
1. 'The List: Murder Capitals of the World', *Foreign Policy Magazine*, 29 September 2008. See www.foreignpolicy.com/articles/2008/09/28/the_list_murder_capitals_of_the_world, accessed 7 January 2010.
2. The Laws of the Indies was a set of laws – inclusive of urban planning – used by the Spanish Crown to be applied in all its colonised settlements.
3. President of Venezuela in tumultuous post-independence times who brought radical changes and development in his three periods of autocratic governance.
4. Not only the Unidad 2 de Diciembre, but also Villanueva's City University of Caracas (1940–60/UNESCO World Heritage Site), houses by Gio Ponti and Richard Neutra, and a profuse catalogue of impressive Modern architecture were defining the skyline of an oil-rich emergent metropolis currently nicknamed 'Heaven's Branch on Earth'.

Anthony Burke

ENERGY TERRITORIES

As typified by the Middle East, sites of high-energy production, particularly oil, tend to be pressure points for conflict. Here, guest-editor **Anthony Burke** underlines 'the slow trauma' or 'catastrophe in waiting' of the unsustainable energy-consuming Australian suburbs.

According to the Australian Bureau of Statistics' 2009 figures, new Australian homes are on average the largest in the world, mirroring the 15 per cent increase in Australian energy usage over the last six years.[1] The Australian energy-production system that services these homes, like that of most advanced countries, operates through state-controlled network infrastructures delivering energy from relatively few commercial energy providers. Although the network is extensive and well entrenched – it has a high degree of connectivity and is resilient – it has changed from a model of centralised control to a highly distributed but coordinated control model enabled by the technological protocols that give the network its coherence. We are beyond formally legible asymmetrical systems of power characterised by hierarchical sovereign states versus networked guerilla-style insurgencies. Instead, highly distributed systems typically deployed as a foil to hierarchical and centralised organisational power structures are ubiquitous or, in the words of Galloway and Thacker: 'Networks and sovereignty are *not* incompatible.[2] This is a pattern that is repeated through telecommunications infrastructures, news agencies, transport networks and food distribution chains.

The slow trauma produced by the 'catastrophe in waiting' of the unsustainable energy-consuming Australian suburbs is unlike other more obvious catastrophic events that mark their moment with global media coverage, UN statements, global pledges of financial support and the awakening of the predatory capital systems that feed on them. Rather, it is typical of the deeply rooted complex networked systems of protected first-world economies, and has more of a cancerous than a catastrophic expression. In this sense, the adaptive network is the organisational form of contemporary trauma, eschewing traditional forms of direct resistance and confrontation through a cloud of impenetrable complexity and a decentralised corpus. The network is the environment.

However, life lived with the explicit expression of catastrophe, or facing the systemically traumatic, is unlivable. Catastrophe and the trauma it induces, in first-world terms, is recognised as a media construction that tantalises and entertains, yet is only possible in newscasts and movie sets with resurrection narratives and satisfying conclusions. Entrenched lifestyle

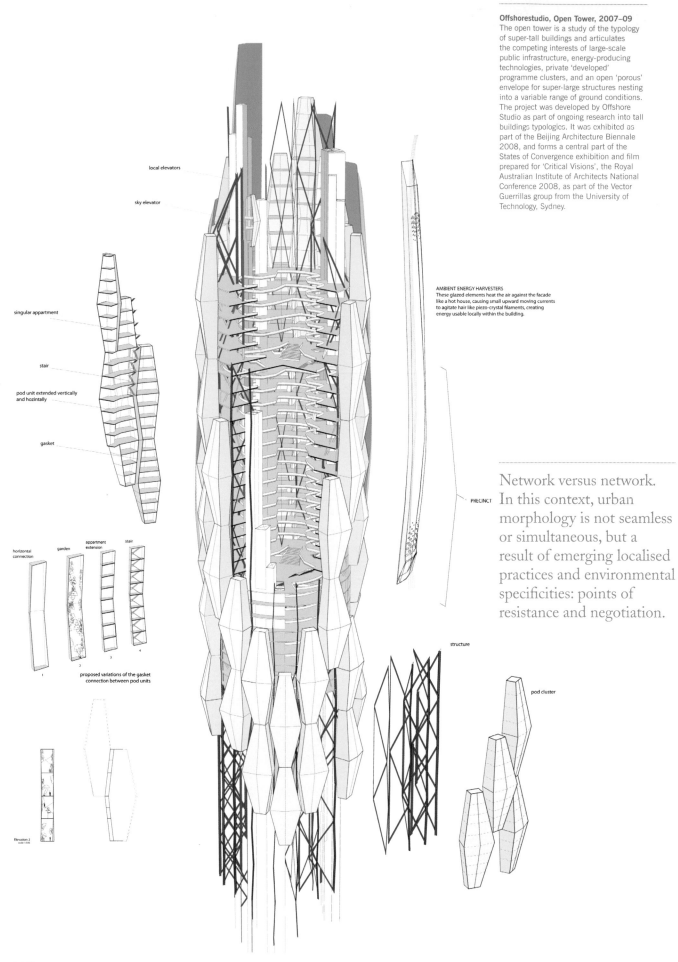

local elevators

sky elevator

singular appartment

stair

pod unit extended vertically
and hozintally

gasket

horizontal
connection

garden

appartment
extension

stair

1   2   3   4

proposed variations of the gasket
connection between pod units

Elevation 2
scale 1/500

Offshorestudio, Open Tower, 2007–09
The open tower is a study of the typology
of super-tall buildings and articulates
the competing interests of large-scale
public infrastructure, energy-producing
technologies, private 'developed'
programme clusters, and an open 'porous'
envelope for super-large structures nesting
into a variable range of ground conditions.
The project was developed by Offshore
Studio as part of ongoing research into tall
buildings typologies. It was exhibited as
part of the Beijing Architecture Biennale
2008, and forms a central part of the
States of Convergence exhibition and film
prepared for 'Critical Visions', the Royal
Australian Institute of Architects National
Conference 2008, as part of the Vector
Guerrillas group from the University of
Technology, Sydney.

AMBIENT ENERGY HARVESTERS
These glazed elements heat the air against the facade
like a hot house, causing small upward moving currents
to agitate hair like piezo-crystal filaments, creating
energy usable locally within the building.

PRECINCT

Network versus network.
In this context, urban
morphology is not seamless
or simultaneous, but a
result of emerging localised
practices and environmental
specificities: points of
resistance and negotiation.

structure

pod cluster

Vector Guerrillas, States of Convergence Exhibition Panel, 'Critical Visions' Exhibition, Sydney, 2008
If it is accepted that 80 per cent of the building fabric of 2050 already exists, the uneasy tension between the small proportion of new hybridised infrastructures and their low- to mid-scale 'unsustainable' context challenges traditional notions of 'fit' at varying scales. Energy-producing facades flip the commercial logic of facade design from area optimisation (minimal surface area) to maximum surface area for maximum energy production. The Vector Guerrillas are an ad hoc team of staff and students from the School of Architecture and the Master of Animation programme at the University of Technology, Sydney, who assembled in 2008 to respond to a call to imagine the future of the Australian suburb in 2050 as part of the Royal Australian Institute of Architects' 'Critical Visions' exhibition.

stereotypes (habit) controlled through markets of desire (aspiration) conspire structurally to preclude the presence of large-scale low-probability events (like the energy crisis) as a conscious possibility. Its probability must be suppressed if life is to be lived in the image of the market, without paranoia and fear, requiring the sublimation of catastrophe's possibility, and in this way systematising trauma and its consequences. Buried anxieties crafting an unconscious slow violence is the everyday landscape of the post-traumatic.

Bringing energy networks and the slow trauma of the suburban Australian landscape together, the strategy developed at the University of Technology in Sydney for States of Convergence,[3] a speculative project was completed by a group of academics and students known as the Vector Guerrillas for exhibition and presentation at the Royal Australian Institute of Architects National Conference in 2008. The project used exhibition boards and a short film to focus specifically on the trend towards converging networks of massively distributed energy and information production, their hybridisation with publicly oriented programme, and ultimately their urban effects. As localised energy production integrates with other material and financial systems, becoming cost effective at smaller and smaller scales, energy has the capacity to operate virally, offering a means of exorcising the systemisation of trauma by reflecting the distributed network of protocological control back onto itself. Network versus network. In this context, urban morphology is not seamless or simultaneous, but a result of emerging localised practices and environmental specificities: points of resistance and negotiation. ⚙

Notes
1. Australian Bureau of Statistics, see www.abs.gov.au/AUSSTATS/abs@.nsf/DetailsPage/4604.02006-07?OpenDocument, accessed 1 April 2010.
2. Alexander R Galloway and Eugene Thacker, *The Exploit: A Theory of Networks*, University of Minnesota Press (Minneapolis, MN), 2007.
3. States of Convergence was developed by a group of architects and animators, the Vector Guerrillas, from the University of Technology, Sydney, in 2008. It was first exhibited in Sydney at the Australian Institute of Architects National Conference the same year, and subsequently included in the shortlist of screened projects at the 2009 Beyond Media festival in Florence. The Open Tower featured in States of Convergence was developed by Offshorestudio (http://offshorestudio.net) between 2007 and 2009, and was exhibited in 2008 at the Beijing Architecture Biennale, and in 2009 as part of the 'Transclimatic' exhibition at the Customs House in Sydney. See www.youtube.com/watch?v=0CirqcuImiA&feature=player_embedded and http://jakovich.net/states/podcasts/JoanneJakovich&AnthonyBurke.mp3.

Adrian Lahoud

ARCHITECTURE, CONTINGENCY AND CRISIS
AN INTERVIEW WITH SLAVOJ ŽIŽEK

The current and popular image of natural disaster disseminated by mass media is one of one-off catastrophe, the implied view being that these disasters have been exasperated if not instigated by climate change, which needs checking and balancing with sustainable measures. In his interview with **Adrian Lahoud**, the influential Slovenian philosopher **Slavoj Žižek** challenges this predominant view of nature as indomitable and temporarily imbalanced; and in so doing questions the fallacy that the ethical and material cost of consumerist lifestyles can be readdressed.

opposite: Slavoj Žižek was a keynote speaker at the 2009 Australian Institute of Architects National Conference, entitled 'Parallax', which was curated by Australian architectural office Terroir.

An empty new commercial building for rent in Reykjavik, Iceland
above: Since 2008 Iceland has suffered the worst economic collapse relative to the size of its economy. Deregulation of the banking sector led to a debt crisis and eventually widespread financial and social turmoil that resulted in mass protests and the resignation of the government.

If every generation adopts an image of nature that is commensurate with its predominant ideological structure, is it any surprise that, when discussing the financial crisis or the everyday fluctuations of capital, we use climatic and meteorological metaphors? Our disposition towards capital resembles our disposition towards the weather; it is a vast open system that exceeds our calculations. We track its movements but its complexity makes it inscrutable. Within this climate of continual crisis and looming catastrophe, the Slovenian philosopher Slavoj Žižek has pursued the twisting, paradoxical ramifications of the relationship between capitalism and ecology, and the possibility of political agency within them.

Žižek suggests that instead of signalling its restoration, the prospect of climate change should provoke nature's radical denaturalisation. Rather than see it as a self-correcting homeostatic system, nature, he argues, is fundamentally unstable and catastrophic, and so 'the crisis is much worse, there is no natural balance to which we can return and we have to accept this total openness and contingency.'[1] Despite the preponderance of ecological and biological metaphors in contemporary architectural and urban practice, there is a sense that this language only works to deny – at the level of public discourse – the fact that below the superficial green veneer, business hums along as usual. For Žižek, these debates are conditioned by an auto-poetic image of nature that admits of no

For Žižek, ideology functions through concrete material assemblages, everything from toilets and walls to performing arts venues and high-speed rail lines. These objects reveal an inherently paradoxical and contingent political dimension that is typically obscured.

Trading on China's new Growth Enterprises stock market that caters for smaller companies, Shanghai, 22 October 2009
above: An investor walks past the index price board at the new stock-exchange market, run by the Shenzhen Stock Exchange, which is intended to nurture private companies that struggle to get financing in a system favouring big state enterprises.

Storage of climatic data at the National Center for Atmospheric Research (NCAR), Boulder, Colorado, December 1993
opposite: There are 112,000 tape cartridges of climate data here, all containing weather information to be used in computer modelling. The NCAR is at the forefront of meteorological research and computer modelling with the aim of better forecasting the effects of climate change.

violence or excess, at the same time as they are caught in a disavowal of waste that fulfils the 'capitalist need for a perfect, safe, enclosed loop'. By doing so they deprive consumption of its necessary by-product by promising to reintegrate it back into the economy. The effect of this is to sanction our lifestyles while by obscuring their ethical and material cost.

Žižek suggests that recycling forms a perfect complement to capitalism, a mask that allows it to function as before: 'The role of a philosopher "apropos ecological catastrophe, apropos recycling" in this case is to see the mystification in the very way we perceive a crisis. We cannot show a solution, but we can show where the questions themselves are wrong.'

This structure of disavowal repeats in curious ways as Žižek's recent discussion of architecture and urbanism attests. On the level of appearances, official discourse constrains the space of what can and cannot be said in public; however the evidence of the objects, buildings and other material infrastructure we construct around us forms a sort of secret dialogue in which the truth of ideological reasoning is made apparent. What cannot be spoken of speaks through architecture.

For Žižek, ideology functions through concrete material assemblages, everything from toilets and walls to performing arts venues and high-speed rail lines. These objects reveal an inherently paradoxical and contingent political dimension that is typically obscured. Taking French president Sarkozy's speculative announcement of a Mediterranean Union as an example,[2] we have the following inherently ambiguous situation: an economic union of the Mediterranean Littoral is being proposed by the person who brought in the law against headscarves in

French schools, and who has constantly played the identity card. The ambiguity becomes apparent when we consider that the proposed high-speed rail line would essentially form a conveyor between North Africa and southern Europe. Žižek argues that within these speculative scenarios we can locate a space for potential social and political transformation, whatever the apparent ideological origins of the object. 'These things can work in both ways; we should be principled but at the same time extremely pragmatic. Let's not leave to the enemy to determine the battlefield. The enemy might plan something, but let's not say that because the enemy plans it, it must be of the enemy. Maybe the Mediterranean Union will be our own spandrel[3] so we can "exapt" it.'

Taking as a starting point the biologists Stephen Jay Gould and Richard Lewontin's analogy between the spandrel and the idea of a biological by-product or side effect that can be appropriated or 'exapted' for a non-intended function, Žižek suggests that once these legal/spatial/technical determinations enter into public space they gain a form of autonomy from their origins and open themselves up to a contest over their use. It is with the idea of the spandrel as consequence of decision making in another register that we first find evidence for the decoupling of public discourse and architectural fact, the spatial exemplar of which, according to Žižek, must be found in the repetitive delamination of the facade in contemporary cultural buildings. This delamination is the symptom of two mutually irreconcilable tendencies, elitism versus openness, and can only register as one object nested within – but autonomous from – another. In the gap between these antagonistic demands lies a space of emancipatory potential.

'What should draw our attention here is that Gould and Lewontin borrowed the architectural term "spandrel" (using the pendentives of San Marco in Venice as an example) to designate the class of forms and spaces that arise as necessary by-products of another decision in design, and not as adaptations for direct utility in themselves …. The struggle is open here – the struggle for who will appropriate them. These "interstitial spaces" are thus the proper place for utopian dreaming – they remind us of architecture's great politico-ethical responsibility: much more is at stake in design than it may appear.'

There are two possible readings one might make of these suggestions. The most obvious is that the interstitial is a site for the fermentation of emancipatory possibilities; this reading has long precedents in architectural history, specifically to do with question of spatial marginality. There is a second and more interesting reading, however; rather than see the interstitial as pertaining to revolutions, uprisings or protests that spring from the spaces between things, might we instead imagine a sort of ontological *poché* that would inhere as an excess within the very register of design decision-making itself, so that decisions might begin to be understood as having autonomy from each other? This second reading would effectively amputate the hylomorphic tendencies of architectural practice in the name of spatio-material inconsistency. ⌂

Notes

1. Interview with Slavoj Žižek, Melbourne, 2 May 2009. All following quotations from Žižek are from this interview.
2. See Adrian Lahoud, 'Project for a Mediterranean Union', on pp 92–101 of this issue.
3. Referring to SJ Gould and RC Lewontin, 'The Spandrels of San Marco and the Panglossian Paradigm: A Critique of the Adaptationist Programme', *Proceedings of the Royal Society of London. Series B, Biological Sciences*, Vol 205, No 1161 (1979), pp 581–98.

Khadija Carroll La

THE VERY MARK OF REPRESSION

THE DEMOLITION THEATRE OF THE PALAST DER REPUBLIK AND THE NEW SCHLOSS BERLIN

Heinz Graffunder and Karl-Ernst Swora,
Palast der Republik (Palace of the
Republic), Berlin, 1976
The glass-clad structure contained public
spaces for more than 5,000 people.

Built on the site of the Imperial Palace in East Berlin, the Palast der Republik was erected by the Soviets in 1976 as a direct expression of their power. As new plans are afoot for a replacement institution on the site of the demolished palast, **Khadija Carroll La** traces 'the traumatic process of becoming, of construction, destruction and theatrical re-enactment'.

The image of a new father appeared at the entrance to the German Democratic Republic (GDR) in 1976, crowning the city's representational border architecture. A glassy vessel of public spaces for over 5,000 people, the GDR's Palast der Republik (Palace of the Republic) was writ in the logic of national icons. With the Oedipal and iconoclastic urges of the recently unified Germany, any adaptation of this perfectly intact glass palace was inconceivable.[1] The strategy of adaptive reuse has in many other cases proved to be a more successful subversion of previous programmes,[2] yet this site on Museum Island, a palimpsest of German politics, will see the return of a phantom past. Florian Urban has recently argued that a reconstructed 19th-century city has been a fantasy shared by both East and West Berliners.[3] Yet if, as Fredric Jameson argues, architecture is not political per se,[4] then Berlin's continued politicisation of architecture through representative buildings is the very mark of repression.[5]

Through the traumatic process of becoming, of construction, destruction and theatrical re-enactment, this essay tells the drama of the architectural mantle. Phantom palaces, imperial and communist, appear as panoramas. It is as if the apparent totality in panorama photography can capture an urbanism that has comparable aspirations to be *Gesamt* (total). Stills from a film of the traumatic destruction of the Palast (also known as the 'asbestos Palast') appear as puncta in the eyes of those who witnessed the building's trial and execution.[6]

The Palast's own 'dismantling', a euphemism for 'demolition theatre', restaged the allied levelling of Berlin for a reunified yet often unresolved German nation today. A viewing platform that reached the length of a city block allowed this slow tearing down of the spectacular ruin of the former communist regime – 'the last days of the empire' – to be witnessed.

Film stills of the destruction of the Palast der Republik, from Reynold Reynolds, *Letzter Tag der Republik (Last Day of the Republic)*, 2009

'On the Berliner Schlossplatz only the rest of the stairway is left standing. According to a speaker in the senate for city planning it should be torn down with a bulldozer between 9 and 9:30 am today. From the coming year until the planned beginning of construction for the Schloss in 2010 the area will be transformed into a green space.'[9]

Between 2006 and 2008, the Palast's 'last days' were presented to the public. The demolition of this glass box was theatrically stretched and thereby politically leveraged for all to see.

This demolition was preceded by another. The iconic dome of the Imperial Palace, which beside the cathedral towered *Überalles* (above all) and housed the nation's father, the king, was bombed during the Second World War. As the city was divided from 1961 to 1989, the king's palace lay in the east, irreparable. The damaged building was demolished, and for two decades the site, bordering east and west, lay empty until, between 1973 and 1976, the Soviets built the Palast, their palatial embodiment of power, on the exact same site as the former Imperial Palace. The Palast's own 'dismantling', a euphemism for 'demolition theatre', restaged the allied levelling of Berlin for a reunified yet often unresolved German nation today. A viewing platform that reached the length of a city block allowed this slow tearing down of the spectacular ruin of the former communist regime – 'the last days of the empire' – to be witnessed.[7] The reconstructed palace will house the Humboldt-Forum, a new site for the ethnographic museum, state library and Humboldt University. At an exhibition of this planned programme in June 2009, the currently empty site was celebrated from the steps of Karl Friedrich Schinkel's Altes Museum (1828) opposite.[8]

If we are to propose a psychoanalytic treatment of urbanism to understand the current decision to rebuild Berlin's Imperial Palace by 2013, we must go back to the urban context before the

'The edgy concrete cube rising under the grey blue sky in the middle of Berlin, carefully locked, as a house with a nameless horror within? It is a memorial for the sunken DDR, a transitional object for eastalgic feeling.'[10]

The city projects a memory into the gaping block that remains emptied in the wake of the Palast.

rupture, which the post-traumatic subject in this case seeks to repair with a fantastical recreation.[11] The city projects a memory into the gaping block that remains emptied in the wake of the Palast. In the transition between past and future, proposals were made. Hundreds of monuments to unification reiterated the emptied icons of east and west meeting, in a handshake, sphere, or flag.

A student of Aldo Rossi, Franco Stella's winning design for the new building of the palace echoes the desire to reconstruct an image of the paternal monarchy. The dome and facades, with Prussian heraldry, are carefully rendered within a larger model of how the whole reconstructed centre of Berlin will look; it will try to look as it did before the war. Yet a longed-for Prussian past bears the marks of trauma: the GDR and its architectural monuments. An outlet for the development of this building has been opened nearby, offering sponsorship opportunities to any Herr Meyer to associate their name with an eagle for the facade. As can be seen in the image of Stella's design, only the east-facing facade of the new Berliner Schloss will remain blank; no eagles will be sold separately. Yet while belittlingly compared to a mall, this move is in fact not capitalist,[12] but the mode of massive representation prescribed by fascist and communist architecture. In the post-traumatic urban condition of division, where both fathers have been killed, the drama awaits a third building. ⌀

Marcel Backhaus, *Das Berliner Schloss 1945 (The Berlin-Palace 1945)*, 2005
top: Backhaus' oil painting is a composite picture made up of images taken from photographs held in the collection of the Staatsarchiv Berlin. The site, looking east over the palace in 1950, is the source for the image here, along with the site in the mid-19th century. Painted during the debates over the anticipated destruction of the Palast der Republik in 2005, the image also makes the argument that its 'dismantlement' performs the return of the destroyed Imperial Palace. The site has since been razed and is now suspended once again in a state of transition.

Schlossplatz, Berlin, in the 19th century
above: From left to right are Karl Friedrich Schinkel's Altes Museum (1828); the Oberpfarr und Domkirche by Julius and Otto Raschdorff (1905); and the Imperial Palace (and dome erected by Friedrich August Stüler in 1845).

Franco Stella, Humboldt-Forum, Berliner
Schloss, Berlin, due for completion 2013
above: The proposed replacement for the
Palast der Republik – a hazy mirage of
both imperial and Modern architecture
collaged together with Italian fascist
influences. 'The Schloss-decision has
fallen/The winning design, the prize
winner – and first reactions/Happiness,
Skepticism,' *Tagesspiegel*, Sunday, 29
November 2008.

Schlossplatz, Berlin, March 2010
opposite: A thin layer of grass used as
a 'public amenity' marks a pause in the
cycle of destruction/construction. This
green space may remain as such, as it was
in the years after the world wars when it
functioned as a garden.

A student of Aldo Rossi, Franco Stella's winning design for the new building of the palace echoes the desire to reconstruct an Image of the paternal monarchy.

Notes

1. For a full bibliography and list of links see: Alexander Schug, *Palast der Republik: politischer Diskurs und private Erinnerung*, BWV Verlag (Berlin), 2007, pp 363–93.
2. See Neil Leach (ed), *Architecture and Revolution: Contemporary Perspectives on Eastern Europe*, Routledge (London), 1999.
3. Florian Urban, *Neo-Historical East Berlin: Architecture and Urban Design in the German Democratic Republic, 1970–1990*, Ashgate (London), 2009.
4. Fredric Jameson, 'Is Space Political', in Neil Leach (ed), *Rethinking Architecture*, Routledge (London), 1997, pp 367–73.
5. Mark Wigley, *The Architecture of Deconstruction: Derrida's Haunt*, MIT Press (Cambridge, MA), 1993, p 209.
6. Artist Lars Ramberg's installation of a sign with the word 'ZWEIFEL' (doubt) on top of the Palast der Republik is further explored among various important positions towards the building in: Moritz Holfelder, *Palast der Republik: Aufstieg und Fall eines symbolischen Gebäudes: Geschichte in Bild und Text*, Ch Links Verlag (Berlin), 2008.
7. Some stood on the platform to witness 'the last days of the empire', as filmmaker Reynold Reynolds did. Stills from his documentation of that title are included here, yet lose what, as sped-up film footage shows, appears as a biomorphic process of the specialised cranes eating the building. The Senate Department for Urban Development streamed the process of dismantling via webcam: see www.stadtentwicklung.berlin.de/bauen/palast_rueckbau/en/dismantling.shtml.
8. Thomas Flierl and Hermann Parzinger (eds), *Die kulturelle Mitte der Hauptstadt: Projekt Humboldt-Forum in Berlin*, Bundeszentrale fur politische Bildung (Bonn), 2009.
9. The End Before the Beginning of the Palast der Republik', Extract from *Berliner Zeitung*, Tuesday, 2 December 2008, p 1.
10. 'Ruin of the Republic', Extract from *Die Zeit*, Saturday, 22 November 2008, Zeitgeist (Opinion section), p 2.
11. For the critical discourse surrounding the decision see also: Philipp Misselwitz, Hans Ulrich Obrist and Philipp Oswalt (eds), *Fun Palace 200X. Der Berliner Schlossplatz. Abriss, Neubau oder grüne Wiese?*, Martin Schmitz Verlag (Berlin), 2005.
12. 'A Schloss-shaped mall': Carson Chan cited by Michael Kimmelman, 'Rebuilding a Palace May Become a Grand Blunder', *New York Times*, 31 December 2008.

ON MESSAGE
AN INTERVIEW WITH MICHAEL CHERTOFF

For governments, pre-emptive strategies for handling communications and risk management have become essential for public perception, which plays such a significant part in structuring political responses to disaster and conflict. In an interview with guest-editor **Charles Rice**, former US Secretary of Homeland Security **Michael Chertoff** highlights the importance of 'lessons learnt' and informed anticipation.

We've held the safety of the United States in our hands. And now we can do the same for you.
— The Chertoff Group, 2009[1]

So heralds the website of the Chertoff Group, established in 2009 as a risk-management and security services consultancy by former US Secretary of Homeland Security Michael Chertoff. The security of the homeland has now become privately available. Chertoff's team, as his website conveys, is a proven one, comprising 'leaders of the Department of Defense, the Department of Homeland Security, the Department of Justice, the National Security Agency and the CIA'.[2] There is nothing new in the shift of major figures from public service to private consultation. Yet the scale of the Chertoff Group's 'public experience' – an operational knowledge of the dimensions of national security – coupled with a client scope encompassing US government agencies, makes it difficult to hold on to classical distinctions between public service and private consultation in the arena of security and risk.

The 'national' import still plays heavily as part of the marketing of this expertise. When asked about the continued role of the national border, given that pandemics like H1N1 and events such as Hurricane Katrina or the recent Haiti earthquake do not take account of borders, Chertoff insisted on the primary importance of national borders in protecting against some kinds of threat, such as dangerous people or goods. However he also suggested that 'borders can also be impediments to security and response. For example, when different jurisdictions do not share information, the information gap may

actually facilitate a terrorist attack. Similarly, when a catastrophe spans boundaries, like a pandemic disease or an earthquake, borders can make it harder to coordinate a unified response. In any event, safety and control remain important elements of managing a catastrophe. The ingredients of success include advance planning, training, clear communications to the public, and a mechanism for coordinating unity of effort.'[3]

Clear communications have led the Chertoff Group to form a strategic alliance with global public relations and communications firm Burson-Marsteller, and particularly their Issues and Crisis Group. A different axiology of space is revealed here, as the group 'provides the benefits of boutique service and access to Burson-Marsteller's global footprint'.[4] From the boutique private environment, global reach becomes a task of pre-emption in message management and delivery. Chertoff suggests that: 'Given today's 24/7 media cycle, it can be very challenging to rebut misinformation and to prevent rumours from taking on a life of their own. The media has and will play a critical role, especially in the immediate aftermath of a catastrophic event. Providing up-to-date, accurate information and prompt guidance to the public is essential. Government also needs to furnish a unified message. One of the key elements here is to make sure that the media is prepared *before* a catastrophic event takes place. That means using every opportunity in advance of a crisis to inform and even train the media about what can be expected in various types of crises'.

Within this new spatial axiology, a sense of the public creeps back, although in an

altered way. While the public will continue to 'receive' the media's message, those with the means have access to pre-emptive strategies of message management. And these means are increasingly aligned not simply with the maintenance of security and the management of risk, but with the corporate responsibility to do so as a core business function. When asked what particular lessons he would take from his political role into his consulting role, Chertoff says: 'If you look at the events we've had in the last eight years, whether it be the terrorist attacks of 9/11 or the natural disasters such as hurricanes, fires and floods, I have been significantly involved in each of the responses. One of the many critical lessons that I bring with me is the importance of risk management. Risk management is not about looking backward at something that has already happened (although that can be useful in terms of "lessons learned"). Managing risk is looking ahead to plan for possible events, conducting cost-benefit driven planning and addressing any vulnerabilities in the system. Risk management is a capability that must be a part of any successful business plan, whether you are leading your company through challenging financial times, or whether you are guiding a major shift in business strategy. And we must be realistic. Risk management is about mitigating, not totally eliminating risk.'

Mitigation becomes the ongoing business of business. The 'lessons learned' seem largely about the necessity of a shift in terminology, from disaster management, with its catastrophic events – terrorist attacks, hurricanes, fires and floods – to the more neutral, businesslike and strategically pre-emptive sense of risk management.

This makes sense in the context of the Chertoff Group's strategic partnership with a PR and communications firm: the lessons learned are able to be presented as transformational of the entire apparatus of national security. Only in the context of this altered landscape of security could the Chertoff Group be on-message in proclaiming its team's experience: 'We came through it together. And the United States came out stronger. We reorganized the country's disaster response system, so we'll never again see anything like the aftermath of Hurricane Katrina. We vastly improved interagency communications, so federal and local agencies won't be in the dark about who's doing what. We developed a whole new approach to border security and counterterrorism, and since 9/11 not a single person has died from a terrorist attack within our borders. We came to know each other under the most trying circumstances. We came to trust each other with our lives. We work incredibly well – together – under pressure. And once you get to know us, you'll understand how valuable we can be to securing the future of your organization.'[5] ⚙

Notes
1. See www.chertoffgroup.com/, accessed 6 February 2010.
2. See www.chertoffgroup.com/about-us.html, accessed 6 February 2010.
3. Interview conducted with Michael Chertoff via email on 5 February 2010. Unless otherwise noted, all Chertoff's quotations in the text are from this interview.
4. http://issuesandcrisisgroup.com/about.aspx, accessed 6 February 2010.
5. www.chertoffgroup.com/team.html, accessed 6 February 2010.

BORDERLINE SYNDROME

Ole Bouman ruminates on the architecture of borders that punctuate everyday activities in the city like entering or leaving work in an office block or travelling on public transport. But what is the impact of spatial apartheid for those who fall on the wrong side of national boundaries and barriers?

There is no avoiding it: crossing borders is part of our daily life. We leave home, we enter our place of work, we return home. And then there's everything in between: the public transport turnstiles, the motorway toll gates, customs, speed detectors, security checkpoints, electronic surveillance systems, the checkout. When you think about it, you realise that it is scarcely possible to move without crossing one or another visible or invisible dividing line. It is the spatial regime of the modern world, where life is subject to compartmentalisation and protocols as if it were a scientific experiment to be carried out under strictly controlled conditions.

Yet for most of us this cross-border traffic is something that barely impinges on life itself. Of course, the idea that one is being continually checked up on and monitored is not a pleasant one. But for the time being it does not diminish one's sense of self-determination. Your movements may be monitored, but your motives for moving are as yet relatively unquestioned. But what if those motives were to become the object of monitoring? Imagine if 'they' not only wanted to know where you were going, but also why. Imagine if your 'name' were not just a matter of your personal identity but also of your spatial identity. Worse still, imagine if you were not only required to declare that you are going from A to B, but also why. And why it was that yesterday you went from B to A. A world in which the powers that be want to know who you are, where you are, where you were, why you were there, why you still are in fact, and so on.

To lead such a life is no longer to pass through checkpoints; it is to become a checkpoint. This is architecture at its cruellest. A struggle for space and for control of space. A practice concerned with erecting borders and guarding them. A continual definition of inside and outside and a war about who should be allowed to do the defining. A war not conducted by people about people, but inside people. In the long run it could lead to a spatial policy more radical than deportation: exile from one's self. Before it comes to this, a lot will have had to happen in the way we try to come to terms with mass migration. There is so much more that still falls within the bounds of the humane and that results in something resembling society. There is no shortage of historical examples. If not nation building or melting pot, with an enlightened spatial policy of mixing programmes and people, then peaceful and respectful coexistence sustained by zoning, enclaves and, if need be, corridors. If not cohabitation, then straightforward restraint with gates and walls, strict surveillance, spying and other forms of spatial apartheid. And if that is not enough, there is still deportation, the simple removal of elements people are unable to come to terms with.

Despite their differing degrees of mutual trust, all these strategies attest to respect for other people's lives. But there is a form of mistrust that can no longer be conquered by the strategies that exist between community and removal. It is the state of constant scrutiny. Of endless monitoring and recording of someone's spatial history as an indication of their risk profile. For some, a stamp in a passport is a trophy of cosmopolitanism. For others, it is a nail in their coffin. Architecture cannot exist without its borders, any more than it can exist without a discussion about what these borders are. ⚫

Text © Ole Bouman. Image © Andy Aitchison/CORBIS

On an industrial wasteland in Calais, France, in 2003, refugees and asylum seekers line up to receive food from the charity Secours Catholique, which feeds them two meals a day. After the Sangatte refugee camp closed down, an average of 200 refugees lived on the streets of Calais without food, money or accommodation, trying most nights to get to Britain. There were many different nationalities, mainly Iraqi and Afghani, but also Sudanese, Palestinian and Turkish, 95 per cent of whom were male, aged between 16 and 50.

Jayne Merkel
Craig Whitaker

REBUILDING FROM BELOW THE BOTTOM: HAITI

The devastation of Port-au-Prince, Haiti, on 12 January 2010 makes this issue of **AD** especially pertinent, and the subsequent earthquake in Chile shows that strategies to rebuild after each crisis must be very different. **Jayne Merkel** and **Craig Whitaker** argue that, although there is much to be learned from previous disasters, no single response pertains. In Haiti, international architectural talent and expertise are irrelevant – even undesirable – until the social, cultural and political factors that helped devastate this once verdant and prosperous land are better understood. It is important to move slowly at first in order to go faster later.

We Americans are not good at summoning the patience for intelligent planning. Nine years after September 11th, Ground Zero remains an open construction site, and the nearest subway station is still closed. Meanwhile, hundreds of buildings – apartment towers, offices, schools and art galleries – have been built privately nearby and around New York.

The Twin Towers were an attempt to revitalise Lower Manhattan, but the World Trade Center never became prime office space. Floors were leased to government agencies. Space was offered to artists free of charge. The towers themselves were neither beloved nor profitable. Only a hotel and underground shopping mall were making much money. Minoru Yamasaki's lacy, flat-topped monoliths stood on a barren superblock – a mocking rebuke to small historic lanes and obliterated street life.

So when the towers went down, architects, planners, private citizens, civic groups, various government agencies, developers and grieving relatives rushed forward with proposals for rebuilding. The outpouring was as much to prove that we could do it better as it was to honour the dead. There were some who called for re-erecting the towers – to show the terrorists that we could undo the damage – but most offered suggestions (and there were thousands) to use the tragedy as an opportunity.

Proposals ranged from sensible plans for re-establishing small blocks to turning the whole site into a park. Exotic architectural fantasies abounded. A call for suggestions on how to proceed quickly turned into a competition to select a master plan that became an architectural beauty contest. Most of the entries were unfeasible: nevertheless, a stunning cluster of shard-shaped glass towers by Studio Daniel Libeskind was named the winner. Before the design could be developed, however, other players emerged: the private developer who had leased the publicly owned World Trade Center towers only weeks before they toppled, his architects (Skidmore, Owings & Merrill), victims' families who wanted to build memorials, and neighbourhood groups who wanted stores and apartments.

The Venice Architectural Biennale, an event usually devoted to the latest word in architectural style, exhibited additional ideas in 2002. But nothing happened. Years passed while the developer sued his insurance company, various interests tried to censor ideas for proposed museums, and the Port Authority of New York and New Jersey, which owns the site, began planning office buildings. Ground Zero became a political football, a free-for-all. Today one tower is inching forward, and infrastructure for the memorial is under construction, but the rest of the site is empty.

In New Orleans, five years after Hurricane Katrina created the largest natural disaster in American history, thousands of displaced residents are still living in trailers or in other cities. The levees that had been faultily built by the US Army Corps of Engineers have only been partially repaired. The city, vulnerable before the hurricane, remains so.

Soon after that disaster, architects from around the US began flocking to New Orleans to offer their services and ideas. They held competitions for new designs to replace the lost buildings. In 2006, the American Pavilion at the Venice Architectural Biennale showcased ideas for rebuilding New Orleans. This display described the history and topography of the city, noted every hurricane, and when the levees were built and repaired. It even discussed the racial make-up of the city, showing how disasters had changed the demographics. It also, of course, contained interesting, innovative ideas for rebuilding New Orleans. The exhibit was intriguing, but unable to facilitate much reconstruction.

The following year, actor Brad Pitt, an architectural enthusiast frustrated by the slow pace of rebuilding, created the Make It Right Foundation and commissioned 21 distinguished architects from all over the world to design 150 innovative, affordable, 'green' houses. So far just 15 have been completed. Although they were inspired by the indigenous 'shot-gun' houses, few resemble their neighbours. Habitat for Humanity, the volunteer house-building charity promoted by former president Jimmy Carter, has built more houses (77 at last count) and five duplexes for the elderly, but progress is slow. And the problem that caused the disaster in the first place – inadequate flood control – has still not been solved.

In Haiti, at least 200,000 people died (the estimated number varies widely) and millions were displaced by an earthquake of 7.0 on the Richter scale although 20 years

earlier one of a similar magnitude in San Francisco killed only 68 people, and a quake of 8.8 (500 times greater than Haiti's) killed some 700 people in Chile in February this year. But in these places, modern building codes were the norm. The few structures that did crumble in Chile (and were featured on the TV news) were the result of a 'development frenzy of the last decades that allowed a degree of relaxation of the proud building standards of this country', as Chilean architect Sebastian Gray pointed out in *The New York Times* in March.[1]

Clearly, rebuilding in Haiti should conform to modern building codes (the existing 'code' is only two pages long), but it must be done largely by Haitians. It is not as if this expertise doesn't exist in Haiti. Even though 60 per cent of educated Haitians emigrated in the 1960s, 40 per cent are still there. As Haitian-American New York architect Nicole Hollant-Denis has pointed out: 'These are people like Cornell-trained architects.'[2]

Hollant-Denis and Rodney Leon, both of AARIS Architects, won the competition to design the African Burial Ground National Monument in Lower Manhattan in 2004 (dedicated in 2007). Hollant-Denis is a member of a committee of the National Organization of Minority Architects working on appropriate responses to the Haitian crisis. Nigerian-born, Brooklyn-based architectural designer and publisher Atim Oton, another member of the committee, says 'everything is on the table, including rebuilding much of what was Port-au-Prince in another location'.[3] She anticipates an academic conference to explore the course of Haiti's future.

Thinking and talking first is clearly essential. Before rebuilding can occur, rubble must be cleared, property rights understood, streets and roads laid, utilities, if not provided, at least planned for. It is much more than a job for foreign architects with bright ideas sent from afar.

Yet, while Haitians were still clearing the rubble, mourning their dead, and frantically trying to restart little businesses, former president Bill Clinton was announcing that his foundation was hiring John McAslan + Partners to oversee rebuilding, and American architects were coming up with schemes and planning competitions to develop new ideas. McAslan had been working in Haiti for years as part of the Clinton Global Initiative, and he recognises the complexity of the task. Also, US Secretary of State Hillary Clinton acknowledges: 'We cannot be making decisions for people and their futures without … giving them the opportunity to be as involved and make as many decisions as possible.'[4]

Also within weeks of the tragedy, Miami architect Andrés Duany had designed an 'inexpensive and nearly indestructible' 2.4 x 6 metre (8 x 20 foot) little blue-and-aqua hut made of space-age materials to be produced by a Miami company offering to donate a thousand such huts to homeless Haitian families. Duany said they had lined up $15 million in investment capital to build a factory in Haiti that could produce 10,000 houses a year and employ up to 400 Haitians. But no one knows where homes would be built, the size of the lots they would occupy, and within what kind of town plan. Each house, intended for the very poorest Haitians, is to

cost between $3,000 and $4,000, though the vast majority of Haitians earn $660 a year (according to UNICEF research).

In February, Gavin Browning, believing 'response to human suffering is a mandate', set up an architectural competition with some colleagues in his Columbia University studio to 'brainstorm for quick responses to current events' in Haiti. He hoped to create 'a democratic and participatory forum for designers to engage with the issue that architects are trained to address'.[5] But Cameron Sinclair, the co-founder of Architecture for Humanity, who has substantial experience with disaster relief, believes 'unproven concepts can be a distraction to the task at hand. During the recovery and reconstruction phase it is better to focus on implementing pragmatic solutions that support the local community to rebuild their lives, than to air-drop solutions on them.'[6]

Fundamental questions need answers. As the 59.6 million cubic metres (78 million cubic yards) of rubble are cleared, can any be put to economic use? Could it make underwater reefs for fishing or the tourist industry? Are there toxic materials to be sorted? Is the steel worth retrieving? Where will all the front-end loaders, trucks and barges come from? Can aid givers train heavy equipment users? Who chooses where to start rebuilding?

Might a new plan with different street patterns be superimposed on Port-au-Prince? Much of the city is a crazy quilt of irregular lots and small lanes like central London was in 1666. After the Great Fire of

**The Seaport City of Jacmel,
Haiti, 15 January 2010**
opposite: Half the buildings in the seaport
city of Jacmel in southern Haiti were
destroyed in the earthquake. The rubble
here shows the excessive thickness of the
floor slabs and the results of insufficient
modern reinforcement.

**Tent City on the Former Petionville Golf
Course, Haiti, January 2010**
below: Makeshift tents, erected cheek by
jowl on the golf course overlooking the city,
create a crazy quilt of colours and patterns.
Numerous small businesses have sprung
up in the tents – or been revived there –
but widespread theft and rape undermine a
sense of community.

For the immediate future, masonry buildings will be the norm as they are throughout the Caribbean. But most Haitian masonry is shoddy, made with too much sand and too little cement. Must the concrete used in public projects be tested, as it is in most cities? Will that require another training programme?

that year, King Charles II rejected plans for a more modern city, moving quickly to rebuild the streets as they were. Architectural historians have long faulted him for doing so – especially since one of the plans was by Christopher Wren. But the king recognised a more pressing need. The site of the fire was the centre of the English munitions industry. To him the choice – between waiting to redefine the street patterns with grand allées, and quickly resupplying the British military – was clear.

If present Haitian property boundaries remain, those advocating 'innovative' housing, as so many did after Hurricane Katrina, cannot expect that one or two 'model' homes will become the norm. There may be hundreds, even thousands of new buildings, all different. Are there water, sewer, gas, telephone and electrical lines beneath the rubble? Where should future utilities go? Are new easements needed? Most Haitians harvest rainwater, but it doesn't rain every day. Is there a common source of drinking water? A wise old bureaucrat once told us: 'Let me control the pipes and wires and I control the city.'[7]

With these questions under study, we may be ready to build, but Haiti doesn't have an adequate building code. How can aid recipients be required to build to an earthquake-resistant standard that doesn't yet exist? How long will it take to write and test regulations? Who will inspect? Do we need to train new officials? To wait for a code that will often be ignored may seem like benumbing delay, but the benefits of assigning responsibility for potential future loss of the many rebuilt buildings – hotels,

resorts, UN headquarters – is considerable. Would an insurance company pay if buildings do not meet current earthquake standards?

Finally the day arrives when trucks are unloading concrete and reinforcing bars. (Some might also be unloading wooden joists and lightweight panels, but that is less likely since most Haitian forests have long been denuded. Perhaps lumber from the US and Canada could help? But then Haiti would need a new generation of builders adept at pounding nails rather than mixing cement.)

For the immediate future, masonry buildings will be the norm as they are throughout the Caribbean. But most Haitian masonry is shoddy, made with too much sand and too little cement. Must the concrete used in public projects be tested, as it is in most cities? Will that require another training programme?

Inadequate reinforcement is also common, as jagged stands of concrete block walls show. Can Haiti produce steel reinforcement? If not, can steel become a major form of relief from abroad? Much of the aid supplied to war-torn Europe through the Marshall Plan came from American sources and manufacturers. Perhaps Haiti, in a most ironic way, can become another job stimulus programme for the US. And, someone should decide soon if arriving supplies will be specified in metres or in feet and inches – not an idle question.

Another early issue to be addressed is the weight of the buildings themselves. Photographs of the rubble show some building slabs up to 40 centimetres (16 inches) thick. An American floor slab might be six inches. Clearly the death toll was

exacerbated by extra tons of falling concrete, as well as poor foundations and substandard columns. Some good buildings could come from this, but urban Haiti is not the place for experiments. No architectural competitions, no gallery shows. Exhibits of innovative ideas, like those that sprung up after 9/11 and Hurricane Katrina, are asking Haitians to eat cake. No 'zoots' and 'whiz-bangs'. Just a simple home Haitians can build themselves, one for which they can choose the colours and the decoration. If ever Robert Venturi's dictum of a 'decorated shed' had resonance, it is in Haiti now.

Some historic precedents come to mind. The Campground in Oak Bluffs, on the island of Martha's Vineyard, Massachusetts, started in the 19th century as a Methodist summer tent city. As its popularity grew, people started building little houses. All are similarly sized with similar roof pitches, but the invention of the scroll saw allowed builders to fashion exotically shaped rake boards and window trim. Different paint colours and different decoration created hundreds of unique houses from a single model.

The three suburban American Levittowns begun in 1947 were once reviled for their identical 'ticky-tacky' boxes. Sixty years later, the houses have dormers, different shutters, screened porches, brick fronts and shrubbery. Now one of the towns is about to be listed on the National Register of Historic Places.

Some Haitian-Americans believe Port-au-Prince should not be rebuilt. Designed to house 25,000, the city had grown to 2 million people. The centre of the historic capital will probably be reconstructed, but smaller settlements with central squares,

**Rescue Workers, Port-au-Prince,
Haiti, 27 January 2010**
Unusually thick concrete floor slabs
trapped crushed automobiles at a
collapsed National car rental dealership,
making it difficult for rescuers to sort
through the remains of the building and
property it contained.

like those in other Haitian cities, might house former residents more comfortably in less earthquake-prone areas. Pierre Fouche, a Haitian earthquake engineer studying in the US, explained that people move to Port-au-Prince from smaller towns for jobs and education.[8] Surely some colleges and businesses could be relocated to accessible new towns nearby.

Hollant-Denis suggests that squares in new towns might even be memorials to the Haitians who died in the earthquake, many of whom were not given proper burials: 'What professionals need to consider is some kind of "green" response. In Haiti, the memorialization of death is very important. Cemeteries are like little cities. Maybe something like that could be done in the new town squares.'[9]

She also wonders whether rebuilding could offer opportunities to explore African heritage, since 90 per cent of Haiti's citizens trace their roots to the Ibo tribe. Haiti was the first country in the Caribbean to achieve independence, yet its architecture still reflects European sources.

In many rubble-free open areas, there is an opportunity for change. Tent cities are already sprouting in parks and fields. What if you built one model area: not a town, not a city, but a prototype, a hundred hectares, maybe less, something small to study and learn from? We would start with tents because everything else would take time. Many questions have yet to be answered.

Someone must have site control, decide how large the lots will be and how to award title – a process fraught with politics. Perhaps initially a single aid agency can make

these decisions without a non-functioning government partner. The Rockefeller Foundation did this in the Philippines in the 1960s when it created the International Rice Research Institute (IRRI). Filipino agronomists had been fiercely defensive of a local variety that, when fertilised, grew taller and fell over, so after many fruitless discussions, IRRI, on its own land, created its own new strain of rice with five times the yield. The dispute disappeared.

Since governance has long been a problem, Haiti might be a good place for one of the 'charter cities', similar to Hong Kong, that economist Paul Romer envisions, created by partnership with a first world country that establishes first world rules for people who agree to move there and abide by them.[10]

With sticks and string we can mark off boundaries. How big should a lot be? Many Haitian families have eight or nine children who sleep on straw mats in shifts. Can we plan for less crowded conditions later by creating a stair to a yet-to-be built second floor? The Caribbean is littered with one-storey houses sprouting reinforcing rods from the roof, suggesting that a second storey often comes later.

Trucks will deliver concrete and reinforcing bars as tents become houses. Buildings must face lanes wide enough to allow delivery, and eventually fire trucks and ambulances. Families lucky enough to own a car will park it there too. Today, traffic is not organised; any vehicle can go on any street. Can these problems be alleviated in rebuilding? Are alleys a good idea? They were in many American cities. Alleys could accommodate utilities. Manhattan's planners

decided against alleys and to this day garbage goes out the same front door through which the groceries arrive.

Many Haitian houses have front porches, so they may need to be set back from the lane. This means longer lots. Should the houses be freestanding? Since security is a serious problem, should a pilot project have a wall around it like a typical Haitian house, or share a party wall? Where will parks, playgrounds, markets and schools be located, even if they come much later?

When all these things have been decided, we might be ready to invite in the architects. ∆

Notes
1. Sebastian Gray, 'Santiago Stands Firm', *The New York Times*, 1 March 2010, Op-Ed page.
2. Jayne Merkel telephone interview with Nicole Hollant-Denis, 20 February 2010.
3. Jayne Merkel telephone interview with Atim Oton, 18 February 2010.
4. Steve Rose, 'Haiti and the Demands of Disaster-Zone Architecture', *Guardian Online*, 14 February 2010; see www.guardian.co.uk/profile/steverose.
5. BD Online, 12 February 2010. See www.bdonline.co.uk/story.asp?sectioncode=427&storycode=3158003&channel=783&c=2#ixzz0fQxfFBt6.
6. Ibid.
7. Comment made by Lowell Bridwell, former Administrator, Federal Highway Administration, to Craig Whitaker in a conversation, 1978.
8. Pierre Fouche at a panel discussion, 'Design in the Face of Disaster', at the Cooper-Hewitt National Museum of Design, New York City, 23 February 2010.
9. Jayne Merkel telephone interview with Nicole Hollant-Denis, 20 February 2010.
10. Paul Romer, 'For richer, for poorer', *Prospect*, Issue 167, 27 January 2010.

Anthony Acciavatti is an architect based in Cambridge, Massachusetts and co-principal of Somatic Collaborative. His most recent work focuses on the intersection of architecture and expansive infrastructures in the Americas and South Asia, with an emphasis on hydrological and transportation networks. Recent projects include *The Dynamic Atlas: Changes of State along the Ganges River* (ORO editions, 2011), which is also an internationally travelling exhibition. He currently teaches in the Department of Architecture at the Rhode Island School of Design. He has been the recipient of a J William Fulbright Fellowship to India (2005–06), a Ford Foundation Fellowship (2006–07), and was Frederick Sheldon Fellow at Harvard University (2009–10). He received his Bachelor of Architecture and Bachelor of Fine Arts from Rhode Island and his Master of Architecture II from the Graduate School of Design at Harvard.

Andrew Benjamin is Professor of Critical Theory and Philosophical Aesthetics in the Centre for Comparative Literature and Critical Theory, Monash University, Melbourne. He was previously Professor of Philosophy and Director of the Centre for Research in Philosophy and Literature at Warwick University. An internationally recognised authority on contemporary French and German critical theory, he has been a visiting professor at Columbia University in New York and visiting critic at the Architectural Association in London. His many books include: *Art, Mimesis and the Avant-Garde* (Routledge, 1991), *Present Hope: Philosophy, Architecture, Judaism* (Routledge, 1997), *Philosophy's Literature* (Clinamen Press, 2001) and *Disclosing Spaces: On Painting* (Clinamen Press, 2004). He has also edited or co-edited *The Lyotard Reader* (Wiley-Blackwell, 1989), *What is Deconstruction?* (John Wiley & Sons, 1988), *Abjection, Melancholia and Love: the Work of Julia Kristeva* (Routledge, 1990), *Walter Benjamin's Philosophy: Destruction and Experience* (Routledge, 1993) and *Walter Benjamin and Romanticism* (Continuum, 2002).

Ole Bouman is Director of the Netherlands Architecture Institute (NAI) and is the former editor-in-chief of the journal *Volume*, which is jointly produced by Stichting Archis, AMO (the research bureau of OMA/Rem Koolhaas) and the Graduate School of Architecture, Planning and Preservation of Columbia University. He is curator of a series of public events for the reconstruction of the public domain in cities plagued by violence such as Ramallah, Mexico City, Beirut and Prishtina. He has also been a lecturer at MIT, and regularly lectures at international universities and cultural institutions. He is co-author of the encyclopaedia *The Invisible in Architecture* (John Wiley & Sons, 1994) and the manifestos *RealSpace in QuickTimes: Architecture and Digitization* (NAI Publishers, 1996) and *De Strijd om Tijd* (2003). He has curated exhibitions for the Milan Triennale, Manifesta 3 and Museum Boijmans Van Beuningen. His articles have been published in *De Groene Amsterdammer*, *The Independent*, *Artforum*, *De Gids*, *Domus*, *Harvard Design Review*, *El Croquis*, *Arquitectura & Viva*, *Proiekt Russia* and elsewhere.

Khadija Carroll La is a writer, theorist and the co-founder of Look exhibition design (www.nowlook.at). Her museum in a book project 'Seeing Change' uses the Humboldt Forum featured in this issue as a case study of future displays, especially of global contemporary art. Her work has been published in various books and journals, most recently in Object to Project (Ashgate, 2010), Blak on Blak (Artlink, 2010), Curating Curiosity (Rodopi Press, 2008) and Meta-museums in Contemporary Art (Melbourne University Press, 2008). She has a PhD from Harvard University and is currently lecturer in the Architecture Department of the TU Berlin, and the Academy of Fine Arts, Vienna. As artist-researcher and curator her projects have been shown at the 51st Venice Biennale, Sydney Biennale, École des Beaux-Arts, Institute of Contemporary Art Philadelphia and the Harvard Graduate School of Design. She is currently developing an exhibition, 'Ab-original', for the Haus der Kulturen der Welt in Berlin as an off-site laboratory for the Humboldt Forum.

Tony Chakar is a Beirut-born architect and writer. His works include: A Retroactive Monument for a Chimerical City, Ashkal Alwan, Beirut (1999); Four Cotton Underwear for Tony, TownHouse Gallery, Cairo (also shown in many European cities as part of Contemporary Arab Representations, a project curated by Catherine David in 2001–02) and in the exhibition 'Closer' at the Beirut Art Centre in 2009); Rouwaysset, a Modern Vernacular (with Naji Assi), Contemporary Arab Representations, the Sharjah Biennial and São Paolo (2001–03); Beirut, the Impossible Portrait, Venice Biennial (2003); My Neck is Thinner than a Hair, a lecture/performance with Walid Raad and Bilal Khbeiz, shown in different locations around the world (2004); Various Small Fires, the Royal College of Art, London (2007); Memorial to the Iraq War, ICA, London (2007); Yesterday's Man, a play-performance with Rabih Mroué and Tiago Rodrigues shown in several European cities (2007); and The Eighth Day, an ongoing project in the form of a lecture/performance. He also contributes to European art magazines, and teaches the history of art and history of architecture at the Académie Libanaise des Beaux Arts (ALBA).

Tarsha Finney is an architect and urbanist. She has worked in Beijing, Paris, Mexico City, London, Barcelona, Alice Springs and Shanghai. Her doctoral work, undertaken at the Architecture Association in London, focused on large-scale housing projects in New York in the 1970s, notions of architectural disciplinarity and ideas of domesticity. She is now based at the University of Technology, Sydney, where she teaches graduate design. In addition to housing, she is involved in research work looking at new academic research environments around Australia, the urban complexities of remote Australian cities such as Alice Springs, and the indigenous arts industry in Australia.

Mark Fisher teaches at the University of East London and the City Literary Institute. He is a visiting fellow at the Centre for Cultural Studies at Goldsmiths, University of London. His writing appears regularly in *The Wire*, *frieze*, *Sight & Sound* and *New Statesman*. His book *Capitalist Realism* was published by Zer0 books in 2009. The collection of essays on Michael Jackson that he edited, *The Resistible Demise of Michael Jackson*, was published by Zer0 the same year.

Christopher Hight is Associate Professor of Architecture at Rice University School of Architecture in Houston. His research examines the relationship between information technologies, design practices and emerging social order. Trans-disciplinary in its relating of architecture to science, technology and philosophy, this research has manifested itself as a series of articles and lectures, and has been published in the book *Architectural Principles in the Age of Cybernetics* (Routledge, 2007).

Eduardo Kairuz is a Venezuelan architect and artist based Sydney. His work – an intentionally disperse practice investigating the relationships between power, violence, technology and architecture – has been exhibited in Caracas, Lima, London, Madrid, Rotterdam, São Paulo and Sydney. He is a lecturer at the School of Architecture of Universidad Central de Venezuela and is currently teaching architectural design, theory and communications at the Faculty of Design, Architecture & Building of the University of Technology in Sydney.

Jayne Merkel is a New York-based architectural historian, critic, and a contributing editor to both *AD* in London and *Architectural Record* in New York. She is the author of *Eero Saarinen* (Phaidon Press, 2005) and an Emmy-award-winning scriptwriter of the documentary film, *The Gateway Arch, A Reflection of America* (2006). A former editor of *Oculus* magazine in New York and architecture critic for *The Cincinnati Enquirer*, her writing has appeared in *Architecture*, *Art in America*, *Artforum*, *Connoisseur*, *Design Book Review*, *Harvard Design Magazine* and *The Wilson Quarterly*. She directed the Graduate Program in Architecture and Design Criticism at Parsons School of Design in New York, taught writing at the University of Cincinnati and art history at the Rhode Island School of Design, Miami University in Ohio, and the Art Academy of Cincinnati.

Todd Reisz is an architect and writer currently focusing on the cities of the Gulf region, from both historical and contemporary perspectives. He is the editor of *Al Manakh 2*, which analyses the recent developments of cities in Saudi Arabia, Kuwait, Qatar, Bahrain and the UAE as they confront a new economic landscape. He is also completing a book about the early modernisation of Dubai and how that era's convictions determined the city we know today. He worked for five years with the architect Rem Koolhaas at OMA where he took the lead on a series of research projects and studies, combining architectural thinking with cultural studies, technology, media and politics. He led the office's in-depth analysis of the rapid urbanisation of the Gulf region. The work was translated into an exhibition that has travelled to different parts of the world, including Italy, China, Turkey, Kuwait and the United Arab Emirates. He has also worked as an urban planner for the New York City Housing Department and for the New York 2012 Olympic Committee.

Michael Robinson teaches design at the Rice University School of Architecture and is a landscape and urban designer with the firm SWA Group. His research, teaching, and practice investigate both the formal and performative synthesis of infrastructure, urbanism and landscape. Current bodies of research and design include Houston's bayou system and Galveston Island (especially the Modernist infrastructure of the sea wall), as well as contemporary design sensibilities that emerge through the integration of parametric relationships and digital design tools at these scales of operation. He was Wortham Fellow at Rice after completing his Master of Architecture degree there, and holds undergraduate degrees in both architecture and landscape architecture from North Carolina State University. With SWA Group he is currently working on a 3.2-kilometre (2-mile) stretch of Buffalo Bayou that represents one of the most significant ecological and civic green spaces within the city of Houston.

Susan Schuppli is an artist and cultural theorist who completed her doctoral studies in Research Architecture and Cultural Studies at Goldsmiths, University of London, in 2009. She is currently teaching media arts in Canada.

Situ Studio, based in Brooklyn, New York, was established in 2005 after its five partners graduated from the Cooper Union School of Architecture. Concentrating on digital design, fabrication and visualisation, the firm uses emerging technologies at the intersection of architecture and a variety of other disciplines to engage a wide range of spatial projects. Current projects include the digital reconstruction and analysis of the IDF shooting of a Palestinian protestor in the West Bank for the human rights organisation B'tselem, as well as an installation for the Brooklyn Museum which will open in February 2011.

Samantha Spurr currently teaches architecture at the University of Technology in Sydney. She has been a director of the Sydney- and Melbourne-based firm 4Site Architecture since 2000. In 2005 she was a DAAD scholarship holder as part of Erika Fischer-Lichte's Body Performativity research group at the Free University, Berlin. Her doctorate, entitled 'Performative Architecture', was completed at the University of New South Wales in 2007. She convened the international symposium SEAM 2009 on architecture, film and dance, which included keynotes and workshops by Brian Massumi, Andrew Benjamin and Erin Manning. She practices as a designer, theorist, and design and architecture journalist, and her current research focuses on exploring the use of performative strategies from dance and theatre into computational design processes.

Paulo Tavares is an architect and researcher based in São Paulo and London. His work is chiefly concerned with the interfaces between spatial politics, ecology and the media. He currently teaches at the Centre for Research Architecture, Goldsmiths, University of London, where he is also pursuing his PhD.

Eyal Weizman is an architect and director of the Centre for Research Architecture at Goldsmiths, University of London. He has been a member of the architectural collective decolonizing architecture (www.decolonizing.ps) in Beit Sahour, Palestine, since 2007. He is also a member of the B'Tselem board of directors (www.btselem.org). His books include *The Lesser Evil* (Nottetempo, 2009), *Hollow Land* (Verso, 2007), *A Civilian Occupation* (Verso, 2003), the series *Territories 1, 2* and *3*, *Yellow Rhythms* and many articles in journals, magazines and edited books. He is the recipient of the James Stirling Memorial Lecture Prize for 2006–07 and was chosen to deliver the Edward Said Memorial Lecture at Warwick in 2010.

Craig Whitaker is a practising architect and urban designer in New York City. He was the designer of the original plan for Westway, a proposal to bury the West Side Highway in Manhattan, and for the master plan for the Hoboken, New Jersey, waterfront. He is the author of *Architecture and the American Dream* (Clarkson Potter, 1996) and 'Next Steps, Hard Choices' (a proposal for rebuilding Ground Zero), and co-producer of the Academy Award nominated short film *Jimmy the C*. His writing has appeared in the *The New York Times*, *The New York Review of Books* and the *Vineyard Gazette*. He was for 18 years a professor in the graduate programme of New York University's Robert F Wagner School of Public Administration, and has taught and lectured at numerous universities including Yale, Princeton, MIT and Ohio State.

INDIVIDUAL BACKLIST ISSUES OF △D ARE AVAILABLE FOR PURCHASE AT £22.99/US$45. TO ORDER AND SUBSCRIBE SEE BELOW

What is Architectural Design?

Founded in 1930, *Architectural Design* (△D) is an influential and prestigious publication. It combines the currency and topicality of a newsstand journal with the rigour and production qualities of a book. With an almost unrivalled reputation w de, it is consistently at the forefront of cultural thought and design.

Each title of △D is edited by an invited guest-editor, who is an international expert in the field. Renowned for being at the leading edge of design and new technologies, △D also covers themes as diverse as: architectural history, the environment, interior design, landscape architecture and urban design.

Provocative and inspirational, △D inspires theoretical, creative and technological advances. It questions the outcome of technical innovations as well as the far-reaching social, cultural and environmental challenges that present themselves today.

For further information on △D, subscriptions and purchasing single issues see: www.architectural-design-magazine.com

How to Subscribe
With 6 issues a year, you can subscribe to △D (either print or online), or buy titles individually.

Subscribe today to receive 6 issues delivered direct to your door!

INSTITUTIONAL SUBSCRIPTION
£198 / US$369 combined print & online

INSTITUTIONAL SUBSCRIPTION
£180 / US$335 print or online

PERSONAL RATE SUBSCRIPTION
£110 / US$170 print only

STUDENT RATE SUBSCRIPTION
£70 / US$110 print only

To subscribe:
Tel: +44 (0) 843 828
Email: cs-journals@wiley.com

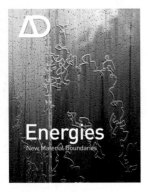

Volume 79 No 3
ISBN 978 0470 753637

Volume 79 No 4
ISBN 978 0470 773000

Volume 79 No 5
ISBN 978 0470 699553

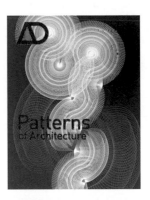

Volume 79 No 6
ISBN 978 0470 699591

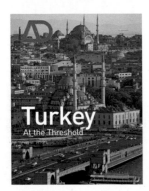

Volume 80 No 1
ISBN 978 0470 743195

Volume 80 No 2
ISBN 978 0470 717141

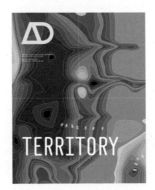

Volume 80 No 3
ISBN 978 0470 721650

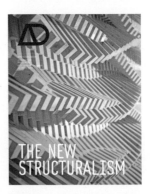

Volume 80 No 4
ISBN 978 0470 742273